The Rise of Silas Lapham (1885) established William Dean Howells's reputation in the annals of American literature. This collection of essays argues the renewed importance of Howells's novel for an understanding of literature as a social force as well as a literary form. In his introduction Donald Pease recounts the fall and rise of the novel's reputation, outlines the various critical responses to *Silas Lapham,* and then restores the novel to its social context. The essays that follow expand on this theme, challenging the accepted views of literary critics by explicating narrative methods and the genre of literary realism. Focusing much of its attention on the economics of morality, manners, and pain, as well as the marketplace, the volume as a whole argues that a relationship exists between Howells's realism and its socioeconomic context.

NEW ESSAYS ON THE RISE OF SILAS LAPHAM

★ The American Novel ★

GENERAL EDITOR
Emory Elliott
University of California, Riverside

New Essays on
The Rise of Silas Lapham

Edited by
Donald E. Pease

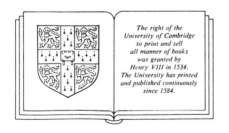

The right of the
University of Cambridge
to print and sell
all manner of books
was granted by
Henry VIII in 1534.
The University has printed
and published continuously
since 1584.

CAMBRIDGE UNIVERSITY PRESS

Cambridge

New York   Port Chester   Melbourne   Sydney

Published by the Press Syndicate of the University of Cambridge
The Pitt Building, Trumpington Street, Cambridge CB2 1RP
40 West 20th Street, New York, NY 10011, USA
10 Stamford Road, Oakleigh, Melbourne 3166, Australia

© Cambridge University Press 1991

First published 1991

Printed in the United States of America

Library of Congress Cataloging-in-Publication Data

New essays on the Rise of Silas Lapham / edited by Donald E. Pease.
p.   cm. – (The American novel)
Includes bibliographical references.
ISBN 0-521-37311-5. – ISBN 0-521-37898-2 (pbk.)
1. Howells, William Dean, 1837–1920. Rise of Silas Lapham.
I. Pease, Donald E.   II. Series.
PS2025.R52N49   1991
813′4 – dc20   90-20718

British Library Cataloguing in Publication Data

New essays on the Rise of Silas Lapham. – (The American
novel).
1. Fiction in English. American writers. Howells, W. D.
(William Dean), 1837–1920
I.   Pease, Donald E.   II. Series
813.4

ISBN 0–521-37311–5 hardback
ISBN 0–521-37898–2 paperback

Contents

v

Contents

Series Editor's Preface

IN literary criticism the last twenty-five years have been particularly fruitful. Since the rise of the New Criticism of the 1950s, which focused attention of critics and readers upon the text itself – apart from history, biography, and society – there has emerged a wide variety of critical methods which have brought to literary works a rich diversity of perspectives: social, historical, political, psychological, economic, ideological, and philosophical. While attention to the text itself, as taught by the New Critics, remains at the core of contemporary interpretation, the widely shared assumption that works of art generate many different kinds of interpretation has opened up possibilities for new readings and new meanings.

Before this critical revolution, many American novels had come to be taken for granted by earlier generations of readers as having an established set of recognized interpretations. There was a sense among many students that the canon was established and that the larger thematic and interpretive issues had been decided. The task of the new reader was to examine the ways in which elements such as structure, style, and imagery contributed to each novel's acknowledged purpose. But recent criticism has brought these old assumptions into question and has thereby generated a wide variety of original, and often quite surprising, interpretations of the classics, as well as of rediscovered novels such as Kate Chopin's *The Awakening*, which has only recently entered the canon of works that scholars and critics study and that teachers assign their students.

The aim of The American Novel Series is to provide students of American literature and culture with introductory critical guides to

American novels now widely read and studied. Each volume is devoted to a single novel and begins with an introduction by the volume editor, a distinguished authority on the text. The introduction presents details of the novel's composition, publication history, and contemporary reception, as well as a survey of the major critical trends and readings from first publication to the present. This overview is followed by four or five original essays, specifically commissioned from senior scholars of established reputation and from outstanding younger critics. Each essay presents a distinct point of view, and together they constitute a forum of interpretative methods and of the best contemporary ideas on each text.

It is our hope that these volumes will convey the vitality of current critical work in American literature, generate new insight and excitement for students of the American novel, and inspire new respect for and new perspectives upon these major literary texts.

Emory Elliott
University of California, Riverside

1

Introduction

DONALD E. PEASE

WILLIAM Dean Howells's reputation as an author was established following the publication in 1885 of *The Rise of Silas Lapham*. Previously Howells had been acknowledged in literary circles for his several gifts as an editor and entrepreneur able to recognize and promote the literary talents of gifted younger writers. In his critical essays, editor's column, and book reviews Howells set the literary agenda for his generation, admonishing a growing readership not only what books to read but how and for what reasons. He successfully argued the importance for American literature of writers as different as Henry James and Mark Twain, and actively pursued them for contributions to *North American Review, Atlantic Monthly,* and *Harper's Weekly.* While the nine novels that preceded *The Rise of Silas Lapham* were, as a result, usually regarded as efforts clearly subordinate to his editorial work,[1] since 1885 *Silas Lapham* has held "a special place in the Howells canon," as Kermit Vanderbilt has recently observed.[2] In these introductory remarks to *New Essays on The Rise of Silas Lapham,* I am centrally concerned with the literary fortunes of the novel, the loss and subsequent reconstruction of its reputation, and the literary and social movements with which it has been associated.

Both James Russell Lowell, who was the arbiter of literary judgment for Howells's generation, and Henry James, who would set the standard of literary judgment for postwar Americanist critics, found in it ample proof of Howells's literary genius. If none of the two dozen additional novels Howells published before his death in 1920 would live up to *Lapham's* reputation, they nevertheless composed a body of work that secured Howells's position in the American literary establishment. In 1899, when readers of the

1

magazine *Literature* were asked to name the ten writers most deserving of entry into the Academy, Howells headed their list. In 1904 he was named the first of seven charter members of the American Academy of Arts and Letters, and at the time of his death in 1920, he was its president.

But in the seventy years since his death, Howells's literary reputation has undergone a series of changes that saw him fall from the status of dean of American letters at the time of his death, to the exemplar for the next generation of the genteel tradition it despised. In 1956 the literary scholars responsible for the first edition of *Eight American Authors* did not believe Howells sufficiently important to include in the volume. But from the late fifties into the present, William Dean Howells has presided over a literary enterprise called American literary realism, as a subfield within American studies that developed out of collective interest in the ways in which literary conventions produced "realistic" effects. The rise to prominence of American literary realism depended largely upon renewed interest in *The Rise of Silas Lapham*.

Shifts in the evaluation of the realism with which Howells's novels are affiliated represent larger reorientations in the self-understanding of American literature that resulted in literary movements commonly answerable to the categories progressivism, modernism, formalism, deconstructivism, feminism, and new historicism. These literary movements discriminated themselves from one another in their different understandings of the relationship between literature and society. Progressivists believed literature an expression of society's aspirations to perfectibility; modernists insisted on the difference between the sensibility developed out of reading literature and imperatives for social change; formalists widened the gap between literature and society in their belief in the self-referentiality of literary forms; deconstructivists extended the formalist doctrine by arguing that social reality depended upon literary texts for its verisimilitude; feminists reacted against the masculinist domination of these social texts while new historicists demonstrated ways in which these social texts could become transformative historical forms. Whatever the differences in their cultural agendas, each of these literary movements found in Howells's realism qualities dialectically opposed to those they advocated. Progressivists found it reactionary, modernists believed it banal, formalists criticized it as unliterary, deconstructivists exposed its mystifications, feminists censured its masculinism, and new historicists have demystified Howells's realism as a romance.[3] Despite their disagreements over specifics, all of these schools depend upon an overarching distinction between realism and romance – one that presupposes the romance's efforts to avoid the actuality realism struggles truthfully to represent – to enforce their claims against Howells. But like Howells's reputation, that distinction has also undergone significant variations.

In promoting critical realism more committed to opposing social injustice, V. L. Parrington, a "progressivist" literary historican writing in the twenties, described Howells's realism as an example of the genteel middle class's defensive reaction against social change. In the 1930s the Marxist critic Granville Hicks contrasted Howells's realism unfavorably with Dreiser's. Hicks echoed Parrington's evaluation of Howells but intensified the stridency of its pitch, accusing him of political cowardice and complicity with reactionary social forces. Parrington and Hicks were equally harsh critics of Henry James, whose self-involved formalism they considered a further development of Howells's fear of social realities. In 1950, however, with the publication of *The Liberal Imagination*, Lionel Trilling turned Parrington's and Hicks's progressivist criteria inside out. Finding them unable to discriminate their ideology from actual social conditions, Trilling criticized Hicks and Parrington for mistaking political slogans for what he tendentiously referred to as "Reality in America." In discriminating literature from their ideological constructions Trilling proposed readings of Henry James and William Dean Howells that called attention to an argument between them over the appropriate way to experience the social conditions of everyday life.[4]

Trilling published these remarks in the postwar era, when contentions among competing political ideologies were superseded by the cold war opposition, and intended them to be confirmations of the necessity to discriminate literature from politics. In 1951 Trilling renewed his meditation on James and Howells in "William Dean Howells and the Roots of Modern Taste," but this time to urge, in the discrimination between these writers, the formation of

3

a modernist literary sensibility.[5] This sensibility, whose immunity from political entanglements Trilling presupposed rather than argued, depended in complex ways upon both James and Howells for appropriate development. Whereas, Trilling proposed, James's novels were expressive of the representative modern wish to coexist among social forms but as if a consciousness liberated from their constraints, Howells's novels were affirmative of the reality of socially conditioned existence. Without such affirmations, Trilling concluded, modern consciousness would be devoid of any material circumstance in which pleasurably to experience its freedom. Opposing Howells's passionate attachment to the charm of the commonplace to James's propensity to enlarge upon it, Trilling drew the following moral lesson:

> But when we yield to our contemporary impulse to enlarge all experience, to involve it as soon as possible in history, myth and the oneness of spirit — an impulse with which, I ought to say, I have considerable sympathy — we are in danger of making experience merely typical, formal, and *representative,* and thus of losing one term of the dialectic that goes on between spirit and the conditioned, which is, I suppose, what we mean when we speak of man's tragic fate. We lose that is to say, the actuality of the conditioned, the literality of matter, the peculiar authenticity and authority of the merely denotative. To lose this is to lose not a material fact but a spiritual one, for it is a fact of spirit that it must exist in a world which requires it to engage in so dispiriting an occupation as hunting for a house.[6]

Without Howells's emphasis on what he called the "more smiling aspects of life," modern man would be susceptible to what Trilling (quoting Hannah Arendt) called the "irresistible temptation" to yield to a process of disintegration, of identification by submission to the grandeur of historical necessity (in the modern form of totalitarian ideologies) which is so much more powerful than the self.[7] If the free play of Jamesian consciousness drew upon the disintegrative temptation, Howells's fiction, in marking the limit of its exercise, withstood the totalitarian threat. In the distinction Trilling further adduced between Howells's real house-hunts and James's imaginary house of fiction, he drew his readers' collective moral attention to the value of commonplace existence as the prerequisite for the cultivation of a modern sensibility. With this distinction between the symbolic and the ordinary, Trilling displaced the opposition – between ideology and the "reality" of America – with which he was engaged in *The Liberal Imagination*.[8] In addition to its political work this distinction confirmed a preexistent literary discrimination – between James's romances and Howells's realism – whose status as an unquestioned literary truth Trilling's moral parable clearly endorsed. Because Trilling was less interested, in 1951, in distinguishing these literary genres from each other than in establishing a modernist self equally resistant to mass culture and partisan politics, he left this discrimination for others to formulate. Richard Chase, Trilling's colleague at Columbia, elaborated the thesis that the romance rather than the novel of social realism characterized the masterworks of American literature six years later in *The American Novel and Its Tradition*.[9] In developing his argument, Chase transposed Trilling's analysis of the modernist compulsion to enlarge upon the socially commonplace into a description of the romance genre applicable to all canonical American literature.

Chase also significantly qualified Trilling's argument. Trilling urged Howells's work onto his readers as a counterforce to the weightlessness of everyday life, but Chase maintained that in American society no such counterforce existed. Characterizing the United States as a nation deprived of the institutions and political instruments constructive of a vital social life, Chase argued that America's best novelists enlarged upon the commonplace in compensation for the absence of fulfilling social relationships. The disagreement between Chase and Trilling resulted partially from the different cultural tasks they assigned to criticism. In 1951 Trilling intended to distinguish literature from political ideologies; in 1957 Chase aspired to define an American literary tradition.

In his choice of the "smiling aspects" of Howells's realism as a countermeasure to James's modernism, Trilling intended to replace Theodore Dreiser, whose reputation in the postwar era was on the ascendant as the literary figure against whom to assess James's literary achievement.[10] Unlike such other prominent Americanist critics as F. O. Matthiessen and Granville Hicks, who found it compatible with American liberalism, Trilling associated Dreiser's work with the Stalinist ideology he found antithetical to his ideas of both

America and literature. "Dreiser and James," Trilling wrote preparatory to eliminating Dreiser from serious literary consideration, "with that juxtaposition we are immediately at the dark, bloody crossroads where literature and politics meet."[11] In supplanting Dreiser with Howells as the writer to be juxtaposed with James, Trilling effectively removed Dreiser's politics from serious literary consideration and literary culture from the realm of Realpolitik.

When he advanced his influential romance thesis of American literature seven years after Trilling's *The Liberal Imagination*, Richard Chase removed Howells from a position of prominence. Because Dreiser's critical realism was no longer considered a source of literary value, Chase did not need Howells to defend American literature against Dreiser's politics. Instead of opposing the unsituated consciousness displayed in James's novels with Howells's devotion to the conditioned life, as had Trilling, Chase proposed that Howells taught a different lesson, "in the necessity of deriving the Ideal from the reality of circumstance, a lesson in the conditioning of the will by the actualities of one's life."[12] Trilling's Howells refused either to represent everyday social conditions as pretexts for imaginative enlargements upon them (as did James) or to lobby for changes in social conditions (as had Dreiser), but Chase's Howells was not in a position either to refuse or change existing social conditions but could only conserve them by searching out this imaginative ideal. In Chase's view, Howells's novels should not be construed as opposed to James's but as unsuccessful efforts at Jamesian romance. Hence, whereas Trilling conceptualized Howells's realism as a literary activity separable from romance, Chase defined Howells's realism as an inferior attempt at the same genre.

Prior to Chase's hypothesis, realism and romance were commonly understood as competing accounts of social reality, social forces as well as literary genres. Parrington and Hicks, for example, depended upon this construal in declaring Howells's novels insufficiently critical of existing social conditions. When they characterized his novels as genteel, the term referred to their inadequate social power. They could not induce the attitude of critical realism required to change social conditions. But when Trilling assigned to Howells's realism the cultural task of indicating the circumstantial limits to a liberated modern sensibility, he denied it historical agency. The circumstances represented in Howells's novels became for Trilling's internal exiles from mass culture formal constraints on their modernist taste for the unsituated rather than political restraints on modern literature. In Trilling's account of it, Howells's taste for the ordinary supplemented rather than contradicted the modernist's taste for the extraordinary. Chase's Americanization of Trilling's modernism completely separated the referent of Howells's realism from its sociopolitical context, turning it instead into the purely literary aspiration to change its literary form. In replacing their sociopolitical contexts with a textual milieu, Chase rendered Howells's novels available to the new criticism, a pedagogy dependent upon close readings of works, rather than an understanding of their historical location, for interpretation. The new criticism's method of reading works independently of biography or history or politics provided a formalist rationale for Trilling's separation of literature from any public world.

While the disconnection of Howells's realism from its sociopolitical context confirmed the prevailing understanding of literature as a self-referential artifact, it also led to the development in the postwar era of American literary realism as a subfield within American studies, a field in whose emergence Chase's romance hypothesis played a significant role.[13] Unlike Parrington's critical realism or Dreiser's social realism, American literary realism presupposed the distinction between literary forms and social forces out of which Trilling and Chase had constructed literature as an autonomous cultural institution. But instead of confirming their status as inferior romances, the founders of American literary realism strongly resisted Chase's romance hypothesis.[14]

Revisionist understandings of Howells's literary career were instrumental in the shaping of American literary realism into a prominent subfield within American studies. In the first of a two-volume biography of Howells, *The Road to Realism*, published one year after Chase's *American Novel and Its Tradition*, Edwin Cady identified the divisions within Howells's literary imagination – opposing the established Easterner to the unschooled Westerner, the idealistic man of letters to the literary entrepreneur, the literary formalist to the social realist – with the more inclusive argument between literary realists and formalists over literature's role in society.[15] By defining Howells's realism against the formalists' efforts to deny his literature its social allusions, Cady turned Howells's literary realism into a counterforce against the prevailing understanding. Howells's migration from the provincial backwaters of Ohio, where he grew up, to the heart of the New England literary establishment, over which he would subsequently preside, became in Cady's biography a parable for the emergence of American literary realism as a subfield constructed out of opposition to the interests of the Eastern critical establishment represented by Chase and Trilling. In constructing an alternative literary field out of the materials of Howells's biography, Cady tacitly depended upon Chase's romance hypothesis as the literary structure against which to define Howells's efforts to produce a socially engaged American literary realism. Throughout his biography Cady exploited the contradictions within Howells's literary psyche to identify its realist strain as what resisted accommodation to an understanding of literature as an autonomous institution. Cady's choice of biography as the form in which to elaborate the case against Chase's romance hypothesis was strategic and depended in part on a belief Chase shared with the new critics – that biography was an inferior instrument of literary inquiry. When Cady restored the context for Howells's realism within this demoted genre, he identified literary realism as a practice at once conservative of outmoded forms and defiant of Chase's understanding.

If Cady found objective correlatives for the agenda of literary realism within Howells's psychology, however, he also significantly restricted the dimensions of the realist text. As the material residue of Howells's psychological struggles, the realistic content of Howells's novels was referable to the prerogatives of his psyche rather than historical fact. Having been internalized as an aspect of Howells's divided state of mind, the sociopolitical context for Howells's novels was reconceptualized by Cady as an inadequate representation of his psychological dissociation. Affiliating Howells's realism with a psychology that refused to convert everyday experiences into a purely imaginative understanding of their significance, Cady did not exactly change the distinction Chase drew between romance and realism but restated that distinction in psychological rather than sociopolitical categories.

Policing the border in Howells's psyche between the Ohio realist and the Boston Brahmin was a nervous breakdown Howells reported having suffered while at work on *The Rise of Silas Lapham*. Cady explained the breakdown in the context of Howells's war with romancers: "Romanticists showed their acumen by fighting it bitterly and thus made the author a figure more controversial than ever. And within Howells himself the backlash of his effort to see his novel through as nearly to the bottom as he could triggered off a reaction which altered the entire course of his life thought and art."[16] By corroborating Cady's understanding of Howells's relationship to society as a frightening division of his psychological loyalties, this breakdown also reenforced Chase's distinction between Howells's literature and his social environment. Having explained Howells's relationship to his sociopolitical context in psychobiographical terms as its internalization, Cady also found Howells's self-division expressed in his otherwise inexplicable admiration for both Mark Twain, who recalled his Western roots, and Henry James, who represented the New England literary ideal. Cady brought this understanding of the division in Howells's literary loyalties together with his understanding of the more profound psychological dissociation from which Howells's reportedly suffered in the lengthy discussion of *The Rise of Silas Lapham* with which he concluded *The Road to Realism*.

Cady's psychobiography of Howells was instrumental in establishing literary realism as a respectable field of inquiry, but his reading of *Silas Lapham* also indirectly confirmed realism's subordination as a literary genre to American romance. As he programmatically discovered the divisions within Howells's psyche enacted as events in Lapham's life, Cady redeployed them as descriptive of the distinction between realism and romance upon which American literary realism was founded. The divisions within Lapham's character − setting the representative of the agrarian domestic economy against the market capitalist, the pragmatic realist against the utopian idealist − when thoroughly acted out as a catastrophic social fall released, Cady explained, an equivalent psychological breakdown in Howells. In narrating Lapham's failure in Boston society, Howells, Cady concluded, came to literary terms with his inability to adjust his writing to the romance expectations of the New England literary establishment. Lapham's refusal to exploit the market for personal gain accrued moral principal for literary realism even as his subsequent move to Vermont affirmed its status as a subfield. In his construction of American literary realism out of this revisionist understanding of *The Rise of Silas Lapham*, Cady established it as the canonical masterwork for three decades of scholars in American literary realism.

Following *The Road to Realism* such notable practitioners in the field as Woodress, Budd, Pizer, Vanderbilt, Simpson, Foster, Bell, Lynn, Taylor, Crowley, or Vanderbilt would endorse Cady's assumption that Howells's realism derived from his psychological experience of social reality rather than his ability to affect it.[17] Because their conversion of actual social events into their effects on Howells's psychology indirectly corroborated a formalist model of literature, which argued for the difference between actual events and their literary representations and by 1960 had become the dominant model of literary understanding in the academy, the working assumptions upon which the realist archive depended peacefully coexisted with literary formalism until the late 1970s, when literary theory radically challenged the fundamental tenet of literary formalism. Formalists grounded their belief in literature's special status in the difference between ordinary language, which depended upon an external world for its referents, and literary language, which they claimed was self-referential. In their opposition to romance as a literary category rather than a historical agency, the literary realists did not unsettle the formalists' belief. American literary realists' collective turn to psychology for an explanation of the conversion of historical facts into literary forms only confirmed the formalist conviction that literary forms should be altogether dissociated from their sociopolitical contexts. Once passed through a literary realist's divided state of mind, a sociopolitical context became a thematic, a set of themes a writer could draw upon in elucidating the psychology of realism. But in the 1970s, when theorists dismantled the claim that any language, no matter whether ordinary or literary, could represent an external world as a mystification of the external world's dependence upon language convention for its realistic effects, they also exposed the belief in purely literary referents and the psychology constituted out of literature's difference from ordinary language as related mystifications.[18] Deprived of the distinction between political ideology and literature upon which Chase based his hypothesis, American literary realism and American romance became for literary theorists virtually indistinguishable ideological effects.

Following literary theorists' argument that every literary referent was the precipitate of an ideological system, a new generation of Americanists have proposed an understanding of American realism significantly different from their predecessors. Instead of arguing that literary realism was productive of social change as had Parrington, or that realism was a materialist supplement to literary modernism as had Trilling, or that it was the psychological experience of the difference between literature and social reality as had Cady, American new historicists have returned realism to its sociopolitical context and argued that it should be understood as a social practice rather than a literary text, polemically engaged with alternative constructions in the production of a dominant social text.

Amy Kaplan has formulated this revisionist understanding in the following passage:

> To call oneself a realist means to make a claim not only for the cognitive value of fiction but for one's own cultural authority both to possess and dispense access to the real. Indeed realists implicitly upheld the contradictory claim that they had the expertise to represent the commonplace and the ordinary, at a time when such knowledge no longer seemed available to common sense. . . . Realists are often seen to take the self-effacing stance of the neutral observer. Yet . . . realists explore both the social construction of their own roles and their implication in constructing the reality they represent.[19]

Unlike her critical precursors, Kaplan claims that Howells's realism is not a function of the formalist imperatives of the literary romance but is instead in conflict with other social forces. In advancing the claim that realism productively contested alternative social practices, Kaplan conducted a revisionist reading of *The Rise of Silas Lapham*, which significantly challenged the reading of another new historicist, Walter Benn Michaels. Because the differences between Kaplan's and Michaels's readings are also expressive of what is at stake in the revisionist understanding of *The Rise of Silas Lapham* that characterizes the essays in this book, I will consider them in some detail.

Michaels positioned Lapham between the restricted economy of a family business and the unrestricted excesses of market capitalism. With Reverend Sewell's pastoral advice to the Laphams to practice a moral economy designed to minimize pain as the warrant for Silas Lapham's understanding of a restricted economy and his retreat to Vermont as evidence for his fear of an unregulated market, Michaels concluded that Howells's realism is a defensive reaction against the excesses of capitalism. Michaels's reading of the novel restored the contrast between Howells and Dreiser that Trilling had earlier supplanted but this time to argue for Dreiser's capitalist (as opposed to socialist) realism. For Dreiser, Michaels explained, "as for Howells, capitalism is an economy of desire, but the utopian alternative, the refuge from want [in a precapitalist domestic economy] that Howells found so attractive, represents to Dreiser only death and disaster."[20] While Kaplan accepted the distinction between market capitalism and precapitalist social practices underwriting Michaels's reading, she argued that Lapham occupied a social position existing between them.

Her analysis of Lapham's social embarrassment at the Corey dinner table constituted the pivotal moment in Kaplan's argument. That scene, Kaplan proposed, represented Lapham's mediating social position but expressed it as conjoined fears: that his social lapses might become an item in Bartley Hubbard's newspaper gossip column for a mass public and that his disgrace has already turned him into the laughing stock of Boston's elite. In her interpretation of the scene, Kaplan carefully attended to Howells's construction of Lapham's character out of his inability to become fully presentable in either cultural location:

> His speech does not have the effect of forging a connection with the strangers of another class but has the contrary effect of distancing them. This scene launches his downward social and financial spiral which culminates in his moral rise – the irony of the title. The

realistic writer then, has the role of revealing the character which Lapham cannot tell himself, and of forging a common bond.[21]

Unlike the critics dependent upon the romance thesis for their construction of literary realism, Kaplan argued literary realism's involvement in a more generalized social project. Whereas Michaels's argument left the terms of Chase's hypothesis intact but with their values reversed (Howells's realistic representation of material conditions becoming a utopian refuge against the actual conditions of capitalism), Kaplan undid the opposition between realism and romance. Instead of affirming the separation of literature from its historical context, she argued that at the time Howells wrote *Silas Lapham*, realistic novels and literary romances were equally involved in the construction of a shared public world, and that the common bond Lapham established became the social glue for a shared public world, wherein contending social groups could negotiate their disagreements.

The historical context for this social construction after the Civil War was not a utopian refuge but involved individual citizens within a more complexly inclusive social change that has been succinctly described by Robert Weimann:

> To suggest the nature of these changes it must suffice here to say that their forcefulness largely has to do with the fact that industrial capitalism in the USA thrived relatively late and then so rapidly that the formation of monopolies and a corporate mode of capitalism, following hard upon the heels of the industrializing process itself caused a break-up of many of the traditional forms of social and political relationships in nineteenth century American society. What is noteworthy in the present context is that these economic and political changes went hand in hand with various symptoms of crises in the substance and function of the dominant cultural and political ideologies, including both the New England heritage of Emersonian idealism and the agrarian and Western traditions of the frontier with its elementary forces of democracy.[22]

Although they characterize it differently, both Weimann and Kaplan have restored in their readings the sociopolitical context that literary realists had previously dissociated from *The Rise of Silas Lapham*. Weimann has declared every element within that context saturated with a pervasive ideological crisis, Kaplan has discriminated its different publics involved in vital contestation over the public sphere. Despite their restoration of this elided context, however, neither Kaplan nor Weimann (nor Michaels) have significantly altered the literary realists' understanding of the novel. According to Weimann, the business morality to which Lapham adhered at the novel's conclusion ratified the values inherent in a democratic public sphere. Silas Lapham's rejection of the offer as dishonest, reasserted, Weimann wrote, "the standards of decency and fair play, thus vindicating the business ethic of the rising middle class."[23] In forwarding this claim Weimann ratified Kaplan's proposal that Howells wrote from within an internally contested public sphere, but for both of them this struggle resulted in Lapham's removal from the contest. While they both situated Howells's novel within a highly contested public sphere, neither Weimann nor Kaplan explained the ways in which Howells's realism either engaged the contested ideological terms or otherwise influenced its outcome.

In place of this explanation, both critics elevated Howells's disconnection, at the narrative's conclusion, from any social context in which his actions could have an effect, into a mythical property. Following their elevation of his exile into a mythological property, the events they described enacted there constitute what might be called mythological supplements to their understanding of the novel's context. Lapham's principled exile represented for Weimann *the resolution* of a pervasive ideological crisis while for Kaplan Howells's dissociation of Lapham from his social context enabled a description of his subsequent moral attitude not as one position contending with others, but as a mythic moral ground exempt from ideological struggle.

If the literary realists previously used *The Rise of Silas Lapham* to reduce its sociopolitical context to a theme composed of a series of oppositions literary realism had internalized, these new historicists have reduced its historical context into the resolution of a generalized social problem. Having returned Lapham to his historical context, they denied him historical agency within it. Having characterized Lapham as able to act upon his social environment only through his violent removal from it, these new historicists have also obliquely reaffirmed Chase's romance hypothesis: Their Lapham does not emerge as a representable figure within this restored context but is expressive of its social ideal.

Their indirect confirmation of the romance hypothesis is particularly troubling. In reading *The Rise of Silas Lapham* against the grain of American literary realism, Weimann and Kaplan have insisted on the importance of restoring the relationship between the novel and its social context that Chase's romance hypothesis had repressed. Kaplan's emphasis on mediation as a key term in her understanding of the novel and Weimann's on the generalized ideological crisis have indicated the different points of entry for the return of this repressed relationship. But at a crucial moment in both critical narratives – their readings of the significance of Lapham's retreat to Vermont – the relationship between Howells's novel and its social context has lapsed back into the state Michaels called a utopian refuge. Howells negotiated Lapham's alienation from his social context, both new historicists have argued, into a critique of its moral shortcomings. Although both of these critics have predicated the difference between their new historicist reading and previous understandings of the novel in their linking it with a more inclusive social text, they have nevertheless concluded that the book's social power was dependent on Lapham's alienation from a vital social context. The composite scene of Lapham's social disaster at the Coreys' dinner party and his subsequent decision to withdraw from the society over which the Coreys presided has induced both Weimann and Kaplan to agree with a century of Howells's critics who read Lapham's withdrawal as a moral reaction against a social world rather than a social response within it. Because the essays collected in this volume significantly question the understanding of its conclusion as a moral resolution of a pervasive ideological crisis, I will preface an introduction of those essays with a brief reading of *The Rise of Silas Lapham* restorative of its social context.

Written twenty years after the Civil War, *The Rise of Silas Lapham* provided a representative account of the conflict, following the transition from a predominantly agrarian to an industrialized nation, between the restraint of self-made men and the unrestrained self-interest of laissez-faire individualists. Before the war, the property the Emersonian self-made man cultivated in himself as moral character was construed as an analogue for spiritual laws revealed in Nature. But after the war the marketplace replaced Nature as guarantor for what was self-reliant in the American character. In this transition, the self-made man was replaced by the competitive personality, who depended less on his faith in character and more on the power of his drives to get whatever he wanted. The successful competitive personality did not rationalize the urge for acquisitiveness with an appeal to natural law, but instead institutionalized this urge in the production of an emergent mass-consumption economy. Interested less in representing emulable values than in exploiting their personalities for marketable sales, laissez-faire American individualists turned every social setting into a version of the market, and the market into an opportunity to prove the power of their personalities.[24]

Silas Lapham is interesting for a consideration of this change in the American self in that he combined traits of both the self-made man as well as the laissez-faire individualist. Lapham moved up the social ladder from his origins as a poor Vermont farmboy into Boston society's inner circle. But once there he depended less on his character and more on his money to get whatever he wanted. Insofar as it depended for its success upon his abandonment of the Protestant work ethic as well as the principle of democratic egalitarianism and his adoption of the ethos of conspicuous consumption and status consciousness, Lapham's social mobility was expressive of his belief in the superiority of laissez-faire individualism over the values of the self-made man. And as we have seen, the prevailing understanding of *The Rise of Silas Lapham* proposed by formalists and realists alike found in the reverse motion of his social collapse a moral allegory of the recovery, after the Civil War, of the agrarian values previously associated with the self-made man. During his upward passage through Boston society, this reading argued, Lapham experienced his social victories as intermixed with moral defeats. In atonement for these moral transgressions, this reading concluded, Lapham sacrificed the laissez-faire individualist in himself, recovered the self-made man, and returned to his Vermont farm, a broken but better man.

If the ethical reading of *The Rise of Silas Lapham* interpreted his rise as a private rather than predominantly social experience, I propose the alternative argument that the self-division within Lapham did not result in the choice of the self-made man over the competitive personality, but that Lapham's self-division was reproductive of the social structure of post–Civil War America. The ethical reading recovered moral integrity for Silas but at the expense of his enforced isolation – from members of the manufacturing class, the Brahmin elite, friends, family, and eventually his former self. Without any other society upon which he could depend, Lapham, in this reading, was left alone with his inner principles. But in recovering for Lapham the character of the self-made man, this reading abandoned too readily any social context after the Civil War in which this self could have any effect. More pertinent to the social stakes of Howells's novel, it lost sight of the ways in which the industrialized society Lapham inhabited had reconstructed the character of the self-made man, but as an exchangeable social property rather than a fixed identity.

In Howells's novel the recuperated image of the self-made man enabled Lapham to console himself not only for his financial losses but for an even more affecting loss of social face: his public drunkenness at the Coreys' dinner party. Following this occasion, Lapham's recovery of belief in the self-made man transformed the social occasion in which he lost control of his self-image into an understanding of the self as a composite social image whose interpretations he could influence. His recuperated belief in himself carried with it the belief that social losses did not merely reflect on the loser but indicated the society he gained by losing. "Adversity had so far been his friend," Howells wrote in the concluding chapter, "that it had taken from him all hope of the social success for which people crawl and truckle, and restored him, through failure and doubt and heartache, the manhood which prosperity had so nearly stolen from him" (p. 359). As an explanation of both his financial and his social losses, this accounting enabled Lapham to adapt to social defeat by identifying the recovery of his character as compensation. But it failed to indicate Lapham's discovery of the ways in which these terrible losses also became Lapham's way of solidifying his social position in the Brahmin class.

When the conspicuous expenditure of his wealth and the social collapse resulting from it followed close upon Lapham's equally conspicuous ascent through Boston society, this excessive self-expenditure resulted in a significant transformation of Lapham's image in the eyes of the Brahmin elite. As was the case with the old Boston merchant class, who were the Coreys' ancestors, Lapham's new social image depended in complex ways on the loss of his economic power. That loss, in having become a sign of his reliance solely on the resources of inner character, corroborated the Boston elite's self-understanding of what distinguished their social substance from the social mobility of the merchant class.

Far from being a private experience, then, Silas Lapham's fall from economic status had become an exchangeable social property able to generate profound social effects. In rising through Boston society Silas Lapham was both an insider (a self-reliant man) and an outsider (a laissez-faire individualist). The established members of society (the Coreys and Bellinghams) regarded Lapham alternatively as a scapegoat or social ideal. Within their society yet different from them, Lapham enabled members of the established families either to project onto him unwanted traits they found in themselves – social ambitions, pretensions, self-delusions – or to discover an alternative outlook on the world untainted by their established customs or habits of mind. His fall from society also affirmed a collective delusion of the elite class – that there was a distinction between Lapham's money and their character. As long as they understood Lapham's rise as the sole result of his money, Boston society discriminated against him as a representative of the commercial rather than the propertied class. Following Lapham's fall, however, the Coreys and Bellinghams found in his character voided of money a social property with which they negotiated more "substantial" qualities.

Unlike other members of the Brahmin class, Bromfield Corey's son, Tom, found even Lapham's commercial interests compatible with this quality in his own character. Through their relationship, the divisions within Lapham's character setting the self-reliant man against the laissez-faire individualist linked themselves with a division with Tom's character dividing the man of substance from the mercantilist. In trading on the differences between the self-divisions in Lapham's and his own character into bases for their partnership, Tom learned how to develop the business associations necessary to increase the family wealth. This social dynamic becomes clearest in the exchange between Silas and his future son-in-law that followed the Corey dinner party. Out of excessive remorse for his public drunkenness at the Corey home, Lapham called young Corey into his office, offered him the opportunity to break off their relations and then in a paroxysm of shame volunteered never again to speak to Tom's father on anything other than the impersonal terms of business.

Most critics have designated this scene as prefigurative of the novel's conclusion wherein the self-reliant man in Lapham morally separated himself from the self-interested man. But Lapham's motives for abasing himself before young Corey are as social in their orientation as was his behavior the night before. Lapham needed a confirmation of what was debased in his character by an exemplar of society before he could recover what was valuable in himself as an exchangeable social property. By designating his behavior as socially reprehensible, Lapham identified himself with those rules and shared constraints that he believed formed the basis for social inclusion and exclusion. Instead of doing as Lapham wished, however, Tom Corey underwent a more complex social reaction. This reaction began with Tom's recognition of his resentment at Lapham's uncultivated nature: "He recognized his own allegiance to the exclusiveness to which he was born and bred, as a man perceives his duty to his country, when her rights are invaded" (p. 211). In experiencing Lapham's demand for a reaction to his social blunder as an affront to his social class, Corey represented it initially as a barbarism, a threat to his civility as well as his country. But just as he was about to complete the separation of his class status from Lapham's self-image, another voice spoke from within Corey that pleaded "with him to undo in him, effect by effect, the work of his indignant resentment" (p. 212) and to protest against the injustices done the Laphams. This aspect of Tom Corey's character identified Silas Lapham's wish to break off relations with his father as a version of his own wish to rebel against his father's genteel social values. In articulating this social motive through his courtship of Lapham's daughter Penelope (the source of the voice who spoke from within him), Corey experienced the Lapham in himself as potentially constructive of a more inclusive social property, a composite character that negotiated their differences in class status into the greater range of social entanglements Corey's business interest would require.

This was not the first time in the novel when two quite different social narratives deployed their different social logics into attitudes that neutralized their differences. Throughout the novel the different subject positions Silas Lapham occupied in different social narratives produced mobile social energies transgressive of any single social logic. He was self-sacrificing in the plot he shared with Jim Millon's widow and daughter, self-aggrandizing in his business transactions with Rogers, self-deprecating in his relations with Boston society, and self-destructive to his own character. Whereas the different qualities of Lapham's character were usually separated by the conflicting narratives in which he gave them expression, following his drunken scene at the Coreys, their relationship became dynamic.

In the events following that occasion, Lapham acted out the implication of his public scandal but in economic as opposed to strictly social terms. As he lost his wealth in reckless market speculations, however, Lapham did not interpret his losses solely in economic terms, but instead used them to bring the different narratives in which he found himself positioned into relationship with one another. Instead of construing his self-sacrificing relationship with the Millons as familial recompense for his self-aggrandizement within the Lapham home, or his self-depreciation within Boston society as economic compensation for his profiteering relationship with Rogers, he enacts a scene that refuses the difference between business transactions and family relations out of which all of these narratives were constructed. When Lapham declines the British investors' offer on his failing business, the net result is a surplus of enabling alienations – from the economic duty to support the Millon family, from his moral guilt over Rogers, from his overinflated status within his own family, and from his crippling social anxieties – which would have the long-term effect not of diminishing but extending the social parameters of his family business.

Having treated anonymous British investors as if they were family members rather than business partners, Lapham lost his relation to Jim Millon's family predicated on the difference between business and family affairs and gained a relation to the Corey family affirmative of their identity. The cumulative effect of Lapham's retreat to Vermont is not, as a century of critics have argued, the moral reaction against a corrupt society but the production of a trust. The object of this trust is not just "the Colonel," who chose to retreat to Vermont rather than cheat an investor, but Lapham and Son, the business corporation that tacitly resulted from Penelope's marriage to Tom Corey.[25] This business corporation is structured like Lapham's ideal for the family, combining the commercial interests of a growing enterprise with the trustworthy self-reliance of its founder.

In resituating the conclusion of the novel within a more inclusive socioeconomic environment, I do not propose a definitive reading but a critically enabling confusion of its categories – the ethical and economic, the personal and the impersonal, the familial and the commercial – upon which the essays collected in this book will variously depend. To clarify the relationship between the readings of *Lapham* in these essays and preceding understandings, I have organized the essays in a sequence that calls attention both to the different critical orientations toward *The Rise of Silas Lapham* already discussed as well as the differences in those orientations adduced by these essays, both individually and collectively.

Bové's essay recalls Trilling's argument with Parrington over the critical dimension in Howells's realism. Seelye's attention to Howells's violation of "realistic decorum" depends for its force on Cady's argument with Chase and Trilling over the appropriate understanding of literary realism; Dimock's inclusion of Lapham's restrictive domestic economy within a more generalized socioeconomic arrangement importantly revises Michaels's formulation; O'Hara's substitution of the self for the market as the site of excessive expenditure involves Lapham in a sociopolitical context different from those proposed by Weimann and Dimock. James M. Cox's essay concludes the book with a summational argument about the place of Lapham in Howells's literary career that depends upon the history of its reception rehearsed in the preceding essays.

While they can be construed as representative of the major shifts in orientation toward the novel (progressivist, modernist, formalist, realist, new historicist), the individual essays also critically reflect on the assumptions upon which those distinctions are predicated. In the usages to which they put Adorno and Foucault, for example, Bové and O'Hara seriously interrogate the construction of the novel's Americanness.

In "Helpless Longing, or, the Lesson of *Silas Lapham,*" Bové draws upon two contradictory interpretations of the social effect of Howells's novel, Newton Arvin's understanding of it as supportive of social change and Henry Adams's reading of it as an "idealization of the commonplace." Whereas these understandings usually sort themselves out into contradictory propositions about Howells's successful transformation of the romance (which evaded American reality) into the realistic novel (which critically confronted it), Bové instead reads Howells's realism as an interpretive supplement to the romance rather than a critical alternative. In forwarding this claim, Bové subjects a commonplace about the novel – that Lapham's failure in the business world secures for him a moral attitude toward it – to the scrutiny of a social theorist from the Frankfort school. After contrasting Lapham's moral attitude with Adorno's critique of American society, Bové concludes that Lapham's morality only corroborates the dominant self-representations of American capitalism.

Bové's critique of Howells's realism should be read in the context of Trilling's understanding of Howells's realism as a spiritual ballast for modernism. Like Adams, Trilling believed Howells, rather than reflecting critically upon it, idealized the commonplace. In advancing this claim, Trilling included Hannah Arendt's speculations about the political consequences – terrorism, violence – of the banality of the commonplace within his remarks about Howells. Bové replaces Arendt's speculations with Adorno's and argues that idealization of the commonplace supported American capitalism's violent saturation of everyday life in the modern world.

Whereas Bové includes Howells within the context of an international debate over the social value of American literary realism, John Seelye situates him squarely within the context of American literary realism. Throughout "The Hole in Howells / The Lapse in

Silas Lapham," Seelye depends upon an earlier essay, "The Rise of William Dean Howells," in which he argued that Howells believed it "was the duty of American literature to concern itself with a realistic – that is to say critical – portrayal of American life."²⁶ But whereas in the 1971 essay Seelye found Howells's realism critical of external social arrangements, in this essay he concentrates on a lapse in what he calls Howells's "realistic decorum." The lapse in decorum to which Seelye refers pertains to the scene in which Lapham humbles himself before Tom Corey. In his explanation of this lapse Seelye depends upon four decades of literary commentary on the conventions of literary realism. In his resourceful explanation of this lapse in terms of Howells's divided loyalties to James's devotion to literary proprieties and Twain's violation of them, Seelye does not find the novel critical of existing social conditions (as he had previously) but an enforcement of their infrastructure.

If, like Bové, Seelye finds Lapham's moral lesson to be complicit with the marketplace morality it apparently opposes, Wai-Chee Dimock in "The Economy of Pain: Capitalism, Humanitarianism and the Realistic Novel," argues that economic and moral categories should not lead to opposed interpretations of the novel, because in *The Rise of Silas Lapham* they are one and the same. Unlike Bové and Seelye, Dimock does not situate the novel within the contexts of either social critique or literary realism but within the context of the moral disputes concerning industrial capitalism. This recontextualization enables her to argue for the virtual identity of the realist and the practicing economist. Because both are involved in the distribution of benefits and the justification of suffering, each, Dimock argues, enforces a model of resource management in which suffering and edification are involved in a trade-off. His suffering, in Dimock's reading, becomes the price of Lapham's edification.

In arguing for the symbolic equivalence of Lapham's moral obligation and the capitalist drive for increased business entanglements, Dimock significantly revises Walter Benn Michaels's argument about the difference between Howells's aversions to capitalist excess and the logic of the marketplace. In "Smiling Through Pain: The Practice of Self in *The Rise of Silas Lapham,"* Daniel T. O'Hara also takes up Michaels's argument. But at the point at which Michaels identifies Lapham's morality as a defense against the excessive expenditures of capitalism, O'Hara argues contrarily that Lapham's excessive expenditures of himself – in the failure of his business and the loss of his home and his daughters' self-esteem – constructed the moral equivalent of capitalist excess rather than a defense against it. Instead of finding defensiveness in Lapham's attitude toward capitalistic excess, O'Hara finds it instead in Lapham's unsuccessful efforts to defend himself against the excessive sentimentality represented in his daughters' romances.

Whereas Michaels and Dimock presuppose the displacement in mid-nineteenth-century American culture of the precapitalist productive self, constructed out of the repression of desire with a capitalist consumer constructed out of the multiplication of desires, O'Hara reads in the novel's self-contradictions the return of the ascetic self within Lapham's consumer personality. When the self constructed out of the Puritan ethos returns within the psyche of the consumer personality, O'Hara observes, a consequent hypertrophy in the drive to renounce results in the transposition of capitalist excess into excessive self-sacrifice.

Like Bové, O'Hara proposes an international frame of reference, comprising Weber, Nietzsche, Freud, Mann, and Foucault, for Howells's realism. Unlike Bové, however, O'Hara reads Lapham's moral resentment as a refusal to be subjected to capitalism's excesses, rather than their corroboration. O'Hara's Lapham does not provide a countermeasure to Trilling's modernist spirit but intensifies its weightlessness. But in *"The Rise of Silas Lapham:* The Business of Morals and Manners," James M. Cox restores Trilling's contrast. By situating *Lapham* between James's *The American* and Mark Twain's *Adventures of Huckleberry Finn,* Cox reads Lapham's moral dilemma as a wish to discipline his considerable energies into social manners.

Whereas most critics have concentrated on Lapham's business losses as the price of his moral sense, Cox gives equivalent emphasis to the loss of morality associated with Lapham's financial successes. In Cox's reading of the relationship between these cycles, the moral economy of pain is in active conflict with an amoral economy of pleasure. Cox finds the difference between these two economies expressed as Lapham's embarrassment. Insofar as it calls attention to the difference between his vernacular speech and the literary proprieties through which Howells condescends to it, Lapham's embarrassment, Cox incisively observes, also allowed Howells at once to resist the Coreys' society and endorse their social reaction to Lapham. With Howells's indulgence of Lapham's embarrassment as his focus, Cox calls attention to the ways in which Howells often reduced the Civil War ideological imperatives to issues of civility and manners. Cox further suggests the ways in which this reduction in a civil society's field of attention justified the relegation of social questions, such as women's and blacks' civil rights or the "naturalization" of immigrants, to the status of backdrop for the construction of a corporatist mentality. His summation draws the discriminations adduced in the preceding essays – between the economics of morality and the morality of economics, Howells's critical realism and his social complicity, romance and realism – into a new context. Here they no longer appear problems to be resolved but resources for renewed understandings of a narrative whose embarrassment of wealth extends to topics – class, race, ethnicity, gender – that await further exploration by the next generation of Howells scholars.

NOTES

1. Overviews of the research into Howells's work conducted over the decades are available in James L. Woodress, "The Dean's Comeback: Four Decades of Howells Scholarship," *Texas Studies in Literature and Language* 2, no. 1 (Spring 1960): 115–23; Kermit Vanderbilt, "Howells Studies: Past, or Passing, or To Come," *American Literary Realism* 7, no. 2 (Spring 1974): 143–54; and John W. Crowley, "Howells in the Seventies: A Review of Criticism, Part I," *ESQ* 25, no. 3 (1979): 169–89, and "Howells in the Seventies: A Review of Criticism, Part II," *ESQ* 25, no. 4 (1979): 235–53. I have found Crowley's bibliographical essay particularly useful for the categories and chronology I have deployed to explain reorientations toward Howells's realism. Many more facts pertinent to Howells's biography can be

found in Jay B. Hubbell, *Who Are the Major American Writers* (Durham, N.C.: Duke University Press, 1972).

2. "Introduction," in *The Rise of Silas Lapham* (New York: Viking, 1986), p. vii; *Silas Lapham* is hereafter referred to by page number in the text.

3. The progressivist reaction can be found in Vernon Louis Parrington, *The Beginnings of Critical Realism,* vol. 3 of *Main Currents in American Thought* (New York: Harcourt Brace, 1930); the modernist reaction and his response to it can be found in Richard Foster, "The Contemporareity of Howells," *New England Quarterly* 32 (1959): 54–5; the formalist understanding is summarized in Charles L. Campbell, "Realism and the Romance of Real Life: Multiple Fictional Worlds in Howells's Novels," *Modern Fiction Studies* 16 (1970): p. 302; Fred G. See conducts an exemplary deconstruction of Howells's narrative in "The Demystification of Style: Metaphoric and Metonymic Languages in *A Modern Instance*," *Nineteenth Century Fiction* 28 (1974): 18; Gail Thain Parker analyzes Howells from a feminist perspective in "William Dean Howells: Realism and Feminism," *Uses of Literature,* ed. Monroe Engel, *Harvard English Studies,* vol. 4 (Cambridge, Mass.: Harvard University Press, 1973), pp. 133–4; and Richard H. Brodhead performs a new historicist reading in "Hawthorne among the Realists: The Case of Howells" in *American Realism: New Essays,* ed. Eric J. Sandquist (Baltimore: The Johns Hopkins University Press, 1982), pp. 27–9.

4. In reading James and Howells against Parrington, Hicks and Dreiser, Trilling contrasts the ideological view of reality as "unformed, unpenetrable, and unpleasant" and unqualified by such intercessions of "mind" as displayed in the Jamesian novels of consciousness; Lionel Trilling, *The Liberal Imagination* (New York: Viking Press, 1930), p. 13. Trilling's explicit observations about Howells in *The Liberal Imagination* occur in the chapter titled "Manners, Morals, and the Novel."

5. Trilling first published this essay in *Partisan Review* 18 (1951): 516–36 and reprinted it in *The Opposing Self: New Essays in Criticism by Lionel Trilling* (New York: Viking Press, 1955), pp. 76–103.

6. Trilling, *The Opposing Self,* p. 93.

7. Ibid. Throughout his discussion of Howells's respect for the conditioned life, Trilling correlates it with the related respect for the conditioned life resulting from Arendt's study of totalitarianism.

8. By the time of *The Opposing Self's* publication in 1955, the separation of literature from ideological matters had already been accomplished. The opposition between the symbolic and the ordinary produced a needed discrimination within an autonomous cultural sphere.

9. Richard Chase, *The American Novel and Its Tradition* (Garden City, N.Y.: Doubleday, 1957).

10. In promoting Howells's smiling aspects, Trilling cannily opposes this attitude to Dostoevski's (rather than Dreiser's). "And even if we take the sentence [about life's "more smiling aspects"] in its worst construction," Trilling observed at the heart of the cold war, "we ought to recall that it appears in an essay on Dostoevski that when he speaks of the more smiling aspects of life as being more American, it is in the course of a comparison of America with the Russia of Dostoevski; that he is careful to remark that America is not exempt from the sorrows of the natural course of life, only from those which are peculiar to the poverty and oppression of Dostoevski's land," *The Opposing Self*, p. 100.

11. Trilling, *The Liberal Imagination*, p. 11.

12. Chase, *The American Novel and Its Tradition*, p. 180.

13. John McWilliams explains the popularity of *The American Novel and Its Tradition* in terms of the institutionalization of American studies. "Chase's model of the Romance," McWilliams observes, "gave Americanists a countertheory of the novel that justified the separate study of American fiction at a time of great expansion in higher education, including Ph.D. programs with increasing specializations in English or American literature," in "The Rationale for 'The American Romance'," *boundary 2* 17, no. 1 (Spring 1990): 73, Special Issue, ed. Donald E. Pease. For an understanding of the importance of Chase's thesis to cold war nationalism, see Donald E. Pease, "New Americanists: Revisionist Interventions into the Canon," pp. 23–35 in the same issue.

14. Cady develops his disagreement with the romance hypothesis throughout the second volume of his Howells biography, *The Realist at War: The Mature Years, 1885–1920, William Dean Howells* (Syracuse: Syracuse University Press, 1958), and he explicitly disagrees with Chase in *The Light of Common Day: Realism in American Fiction* (Bloomington: Indiana University Press, 1971), pp. 196–201.

15. Edwin Cady, *The Road to Realism: The Early Years 1883–1885, of William Dean Howells* (Syracuse: Syracuse University Press, 1956).

16. Cady, *The Road to Realism*, page 240. For a succinct account of this breakdown and the role it played in criticism of Howells, see Kermit Vanderbilt, "Introduction," *The Rise of Silas Lapham*, pp. viii–xi, and Cady, *The Road to Realism*, pp. 243–45.

17. Cady's *The Realist at War* predicted some of the directions for subsequent generations of scholars in American literary realism. He also

provided the field with a formative controversy in *The War of the Critics over William Dean Howells*, eds. Edwin Cady and David W. Frazier (New York: Row, Peterson, 1962).

18. For demonstrations of the effect of deconstruction on the understanding of realism, see the essays by Evan Carton, Walter Benn Michaels, and Donald Pease in Sundquist, *American Realism*. In an unpublished graduate paper Timothy Scherman discusses the importance of theory to the criticism of *Lapham*.

19. Amy Kaplan, *The Social Construction of American Realism* (Chicago: University of Chicago Press, 1988), p. 13.

20. Walter Benn Michaels, *The Gold Standard and the Logic of Naturalism* (Berkeley: University of California Press, 1987), p. 46.

21. *The Social Construction of Realism*, p. 41.

22. Robert Weimann, "Realism, Ideology, and the Novel in America (1886–1896): Changing Perspectives in the Work of Mark Twain, W. D. Howells and Henry James," *boundary 2* 17, no. 1 (Spring 1990, Special Issue, ed. Donald E. Pease): 191.

23. "Realism, Ideology and the Novel in America," p. 203.

24. Michael Spindler offers a more precise account of Lapham's transformation into a laissez-faire individualist in *American Literature and Social Change: William Dean Howells to Arthur Miller* (Bloomington, Indiana University Press, 1983), pp. 1–11, 48–74.

25. Howells indicates the corporate implications of Lapham's transformation into the "Colonel" following his retreat to Vermont in the following passage: "The transfer relieved Lapham of the load of debt which he was still laboring under, and gave him an interest in the vaster enterprise of the younger men which he had once vainly hoped to grasp all in his own hand. He began to tell of this coincidence as something very striking, and pushing on more actively in the special branch of the business left to him, he bragged, quite in the old way, of its enormous extension. His son-in-law, he said, was pushing it in Mexico and Central America: an idea that they had originally had in common," p. 361.

26. John Seelye, "The Rise of William Dean Howells," *New Republic* 165 (3 July 1971): 25.

2

Helpless Longing, or, the Lesson of *Silas Lapham*

PAUL A. BOVÉ

Our descendants will find nowhere so faithful and so pleasing a picture of our American existence, and no writer is likely to rival Mr. Howells in this idealization of the commonplace. The vein which Mr. Howells has struck is hardly a deep one. His dexterity in following it, and in drawing out its slightest resources, seems at times almost marvellous, a perpetual succession of feats of sleight-of-hand, all the more remarkable because the critical reader alone will understand how difficult such feats are, and how much tact and wit is needed to escape a mortifying failure.

—Henry Adams, *The North American Review,* 1872

I

WILLIAM Dean Howells was not the first novelist to understand the critical possibilities inherent in the realistic novel; he had learned much from his European predecessors in the style. His claim to fame, however, rests upon his having been an American who chose to bring these possibilities to bear upon uniquely American materials at a time when, as the critics would have it, the norms of Puritan and genteel literature, of the romance, were no longer adequate to portraying the new world of the post–Civil War United States. Newton Arvin once gave voice to this way of judging Howells when he wrote in *The New Republic* that

he was the first of our important imaginative writers thoughtfully to consider and intelligently to comprehend what was happening to the form and quality of American life as it moved away from the simplicity, the social fluidity, the relative freedoms, of the mid-century toward the ugly disharmonies of monopolism and empire. He was the author of the first realistic novels of permanent interest in which the effects of that development are represented dramatically with any fullness or clarity.[1]

We can easily see now that Arvin typically articulates his judgment on the narrative and ethical basis of the myth of the fall, a fall from prewar simplicity into postwar capitalism and its "disharmonies." Howells's value, in this critical myth, lies not only in the lucidity with which he lets his readers see the dramatic and terrible social effects of monopoly capitalism in its imperial mode, but also in the success of his dramatic representations that reconfigure these social disharmonies into the "fullness or clarity" of a new art appropriate to his age and its successors. Of course, one might argue that such claims as Arvin's should be taken as examples of a criticism devoted to the defense of art as a possibility of human life that can accomplish its own goals no matter the social context. Indeed, such an argument might say that Arvin insists that Howells produces work of *"permanent* interest" (my emphasis). But such an argument about Arvin would miss an important issue that those today interested in the criticism of culture must not avoid. Arvin would have it that Howells's success is the success of the "American" social order. The imperial monopolistic social order is not all-embracing; it is not tyrannically totalitarian – as Jeane Kirkpatrick would perhaps put it in speaking of Nicaragua or the Soviet Union. It is merely unjust, ugly, threatens freedom, and the possibility of social change, but – and the *but* is crucial for Howells's critics – there are spaces within it where it is possible for the critical mind, the artistic and moral realist to shape and circulate the just representations of this unjust and "disharmonious" order. Arvin reminds us that Howells cast off all the "old Jacksonian illusions" and faced the fact that business had become the dominant reality of U.S. culture. Howells had the discipline to take seriously the real, to face it squarely, to represent it clearly so that the representations might be tested, scientifically, as it were, against everyday realities. He had the courage not to blink before the ugly and to develop a style adequate to the representations necessary to give his art moral and affective force. But what of this judgment on his art? How are we to read it?

We could say that it represents a normative liberal position, one common to *The New Republic* of its time, under the leadership of Herbert Croly and the more complex Edmund Wilson. But what would it mean in this case to say such a thing? Arvin's reading of

Howells as evidence of the possibility for liberal reform, as a source for an aesthetically and morally complex judgment upon capitalistic U.S. society, legitimates that culture in a way that is unarticulated and, when read from a distance, hard to justify. Recall the opening of Arvin's remarks: "he was the first of our important imaginative writers" to "comprehend" the changes in American life. Arvin has, of course, placed Howells within a continuing chain of "important imaginative writers," a placing that deflects praise from that chain and the culture that it links to the writers added to it. But always unspoken is the ideological commitment to the value of America and to the fact that it can produce and sustain, that it can make a chain of, important imaginative writers who are its critics, who "comprehend" its ugliness, brutality, and empire-building. It is hard to comprehend how a critic like Arvin could come to transfer the values of a culture grown disharmonious to an imaginative writer who is its critic; it is hard to imagine until one sees that this critical, journalistic move is itself part of the ideological operations of the problematic American nation. It is more than a double move: Value inheres in America (who could doubt this in any final way?); part of that value is in its array of imaginative writers cultivated by the culture, cultivators of it.[2] In turn the existence of this chain within a culture requires comprehensive representation so that its novelty, its modernity might be seen. This existence paradoxically legitimates even that culture which, as Howells's novel so effectively shows, needs imaginative evaluation and correction.

Arvin's remarks on Howells would be interesting in themselves as an example of the efforts made by U.S. critics to give their literature a legitimating function within a society thought – despite its worst effects – to need little justification. One need only recall some of Henry James's remarks on Howells to remember that even that most valiant critic of America and its poverty of imaginative resources cannot quite let go of the values America stands for in its own myths:

> The American life when he [Howells] for the most part depicts it is certainly neither very rich nor very fair, but it is tremendously positive. . . . He is animated by a love of the common, the immediate, the familiar and vulgar elements of life, and holds that in pro-

portion as we move into the rare and strange we become vague and arbitrary; that the truth of representation, in a word, can be achieved only so long as it is in our power to test and measure it. He thinks scarcely anything too paltry to be interesting, that the small and the vulgar have been terribly neglected, and would rather see an exact account of a sentiment or a character he stumbles against every day than a brilliant evocation of a passion or a type that he has never seen and does not even particularly believe in. He adores the real, the natural, the colloquial, the moderate, the optimistic, the domestic, and the democratic.[3]

Indeed, it is in the name of the democratic possibilities of the common man that Howells's realism is defended. Lapham himself, as a common man almost destroyed by success within the new capitalist order of near monopoly production, can but be read as the allegory of the democratic ideal in American ideology, a fate destined to succeed when it fulfills its best self, on the basis of its reserves of timeless humanity and past values, from the threatening disharmonies of the newly modern present. Howells's realism is like the drawing on these reserves; it is a "recollection" for a present that cannot find within itself the capacity to let anything other than "business" become the leading force for "modernization" in the culture. At least that is how the critics that favor Howells must generally tell the story.

II

There have been readers who have wished that Howells was not so fascinated with such recurrent figures as Bromfield Corey, feeling that his inability to give them up is a mark of his Boston provinciality, of the narrowness of his experience and imaginative vision. They may well be right. In *The Rise of Silas Lapham*, though, the Coreys and Bromfield especially are much more interesting than usual. In an important way, Bromfield Corey should be read as set off and over against not the figure of Colonel Lapham himself, but rather his ever redoubtable and puritanical wife, Persis. Howells sets up a dramatic contrast between two forms of tradition, two forms of moral and aesthetic reserve, both recollected in the Boston of his novel's present, but neither really very much able to deal with its modern complexities; indeed, as we see, both easily bring about disaster and wander in perplexity.

Bromfield Corey is a pale shadow of a Kierkegaardian ironist, a faded seducer, a not-quite Knight of Infinite Resignation, a not-quite ascetic idealist. He is not Abraham, nor Marius, nor Dorian. He is an American echo of those types: "'We represent a faded tradition.' He says to his wife, 'We don't really care what business a man is in, so it is large enough, and he doesn't advertise offensively; but we think it fine to affect reluctance.' "[4] In Chapter V, the exchange between Corey *père* and *fils* actually casts the difference between the two in terms of difference of reserve. One has a Roman nose and so energy – the inheritance from a grandfather – the other has a "straight nose" (p. 69) and lacks energy; he becomes a gentleman, a traveler, and a dilettante. Tom Corey recovers some of the old "India merchant's" moneymaking desires to be independent and self-made. His type lies at the origin of Brahmin and genteel society. But Bromfield has had access to reserves of a different sort: voyages to Europe, learning, leisure, and "culture." He still reads the *Revue des deux mondes*. But this reserve has become little more than whimsy (p. 69), a stooped amusement at his son's unwillingness to tolerate the inconvenience of feudal virtues in a modern society (p. 67). Uncle Jim is a sign in the novel of how the genteel folk can continue to have some well-mannered head for business, but his character hasn't the prominence or point of Bromfield's.

In Chapter VIII, Bromfield's persistent exhaustion appears in conversation with his wife about Tom's chances. The chapter develops Bromfield's character quite literally in terms of the declining values of its shrinking reserves: The decline of his family's financial position is told in parallel to his wife's "recollection" of his life since their marriage. That Corey is a persistent remainder of a previous type of social life, Howells clearly stresses; but that it is a form adaptable to modern life – able to survive within it, but unable to affect it – Howells also makes clear:

> "I don't see how you can joke about such things, Bromfield," she added. "Well, I don't either, my dear, to tell you the truth. My hardiness surprises me. Here is a son of mine whom I see reduced to making his living by a shrinkage in values. It's very odd," interjected

Corey, "that some values should have this peculiarity of shrinking. You never hear of values in a picture shrinking; but rents, stocks, real estate – all those values shrink abominably. Perhaps it might be argued that one should put all his values into pictures; I've got a good many of mine there." (pp. 95–6)

All of this recalls Chapter V's conclusion, the brief account of the Coreys' quite typical financial failures: "In process of time the money seemed less abundant. There were shrinkages of one kind and another, and living had grown more expensive and luxurious" (p. 70). But when Mrs. Corey recalls the life of Bromfield, a life that is not paradoxically a story of decline, but of successful fulfillment, we can see what must happen to this pale aesthete, this weak shadow of the bolder figures in Kierkegaard, Pater, Wilde, and others. Bromfield had seduced the young woman who became his wife by saying "just the things to please the fancy of a girl who was disposed to take life a little too seriously and practically." Of course, after the wedding he did no more than talk, putting aside even his talents as an amateur portraitist. He is fiscally conservative, but from apathy rather than scruples and "In the process of time he had grown to lead a more and more secluded life." Mrs. Corey assigns "pathos" as a value to Bromfield's narrowed life, but he gives it another name when he discusses his son's chances for marriage: "The right way is for us to school ourselves to indifference. . . . It is absurd for us to have any feelings about what we don't interfere with. . . . the only motto for us is, Hands off altogether" (pp. 96–7).

By contrast Mrs. Lapham is capable of no indifference at all. Howells repeatedly tells us that her morality is Puritan, country, and traditional in kind and origin. She is always the conscience to Lapham, especially in the Rogers affair:

> He had been dependent at one time on his partner's capital. It was a moment of terrible trial. Happy is the man forever who can choose the ideal, the unselfish part in such an exigency! Lapham could not rise to it. He did what he could maintain to be perfectly fair. The wrong, if any, seemed to be condoned to him, except when from time to time his wife brought it up. Then all the question stung and burned anew, and had to be reasoned out and put away once more. It seemed to have an inextinguishable vitality. It slept, but it did not die. (p. 50)

As Howells constructs his characters and their dilemmas, we see that Lapham's success depends upon his being an obsessive mind, a personality unable to define itself except in terms of a fixed idea that has all the passion of poetry and all the compulsion of survival to him — while to most others at most times it seems boring and prosaic. And, of course, it is just in the poetry of his passion that Lapham is morally vulnerable; for otherwise "blameless in all his life" (p. 50), Lapham can commit wrong only when driven by his self-defining, repressive, and essential passion. As Howells tells the story, the consequences of this passion and its repressive energies are disastrous financially as the repressed returns; but the very return is the ground for renewal, for a return to simple country origins, to a past rediscovered, full now not with the false promises of wealth, but the stable almost kulak-like security of farm and small business. And, of course, the key to this return and the reserves that are validated by its success are the best of those values represented by Mrs. Lapham, especially when we see them enacted on the basis of Lapham's own natural moral courage.

The two most remarkable elements of the novel involving Mrs. Lapham are, of course, her prodding Lapham to make amends to Rogers, a prodding that, in part, leads to their financial collapse; and her mistakes in understanding Tom Corey's intentions. In urging penance on Lapham for his rough use of Rogers, Persis shows the strongest of her virtues; it is a strength she comes to regret but cannot supersede. Having been told how bad their financial situation is, Mrs. Lapham responds this way: "'I know who's to blame, and I blame myself. It was my forcing Rogers on to you.' She came back to this, with her helpless longing, inbred in all Puritan souls, to have some one specifically suffer for the evil in the world, even if it must be herself" (p. 277). Of course, Howells's narrator is never very harsh on this woman who has moral reserves no less than almost any other person. Indeed, although she never comes to supersede the limits of her Puritanism, she comes to see the moral trap lying baited for the successful moral consciences:

> She had passed the day in a passion of self-reproach . . . and now she could wait no longer to tell him that she saw how she had forsaken him. . . . She wondered at herself in shame and dismay. . . . if there was any virtue upon which this good woman

prided herself, in which she thought herself superior to her husband, it was her instant and steadfast perception of right and wrong, and the ability to choose the right to her own hurt. But now she had to confess, as each of us has had likewise to confess in his own case, that the very virtue on which she prided herself was the thing that had played her false. (p. 334)

Of course, as Persis and the narrator tell us, it is Lapham's victory to have wrestled with the angel (p. 331) and to have gone beyond the moral position to which his wife had brought him; Persis "admired and revered him for going beyond her" (p. 335). We remember, however, that achieving this newfound admiration does not prevent Persis from jealously suspecting her husband of adultery just a short number of lines later (p. 337).

In both subplots that involve Persis, we see that Howells uses her to present basic virtues appropriate to her gender and her small-town, schoolteacher origins, virtues that can warn her family members of many impending problems and difficulties. She is a very weak shade of both Virgil and Beatrice in Dante. But we also see that these very virtues that belong to the small-town past of Persis's life collapse in the face of novel crises, and we have no doubt that Howells would have us see how limited in the new circumstances of modern Boston her traditional rural values actually are. On visiting Minister Sewell for advice about the Tom Corey affair, the narrator tells us that Persis could not imagine that anyone else had ever been in a situation like hers before. That she is limited in her capacity for imaginative sympathy causes many of the problems in the two affairs in which she figures prominently. Howells's narrator would have his readers understand the suffering of her position while seeing, too, its inadequacy as a moral and social mode of being: "'Was there ever any poor creatures in such a strait before?' she asked [Sewell], with pathetic incredulity" (p. 240). Perhaps the limitations of Persis's character emerge from Howells's problems in imagining women, including Penelope, who have the natural moral reserve of some of his men, most importantly, Lapham himself. No doubt, Howells finds it easy to make women, in this case Persis, the marked bearer of past, rigid, and collapsed value systems that float free of any tie to the moral power of the natural goodness we see in Lapham. Even Penelope, we must remember, does not escape the narrator's censure in this scene with Sewell. She has been reading "Tears, Idle Tears" and unthinkingly transfers the self-destructive "solutions" of that romance to her own triangular relationship with Tom and Irene. Sewell analyzes Penelope's failure to see her situation clearly in a way that echoes many of Howells's own fictional and critical animadversions on nonrealistic fiction. Interestingly, Sewell's position converges with one expressed earlier by Bromfield Corey (p. 118). Sewell puts the case for "common-sense" as opposed to the values and effects of imaginative literature: "I don't know," he says to the Laphams, "where this false ideal comes from, unless it comes from the novels that befool and debauch almost every intelligence in some degree" (p. 241).

We expect the realist, Howells, to regret literature that implants "false ideals," that paints pictures of the fantastic that cannot be checked. Indeed, we are to see that he "realistically" portrays the reading habits of some young women as they respond to "Tears, Idle Tears." A Corey daughter, sophisticated no doubt by travel and time spent in her father's study, renames the novel "Slop, Silly Slop." A dinner guest gushes tears over the heroic "self-sacrifice" of its main characters. Penelope tells us the novel moves her and yet, although sentimental, is plainly natural, but surprisingly affronts common sense. What are we to make of these novels?

The Puritan voice of Mrs. Lapham gives us the standard position: "'She reads a great deal,' admitted her mother. 'She seems to be at it the whole while. . . . I don't know as it's good for a girl to read so much, anyway, especially novels. I don't want she should get notions' " (p. 135). Persis's opinion, which could be a sad gloss on Emma Bovary's fate, is more naive than Mr. Sewell's. He would welcome literature's aid in forging Christian souls; he sounds like the Howells the critics have given us: "The novelists might be the greatest possible help to us if they painted life as it is, and human feelings in their true proportion and relation, but for the most part they have been and are altogether noxious" (p. 197). This "true proportion and relation" reminds us, in part, of Arvin's "thoughtfully to consider and intelligently to comprehend" the complex life in modern U.S. society. "Tears, Idle Tears" should hardly, then, be the sort of book one would expect to find Howells's narrator praising; yet, no less an authority than Penelope gives us a reason not easily to dismiss the book. When Corey asks ironically if Penelope had cried over the romance, she responds this way: "Oh, it's pretty easy to cry over a book . . . and that one *is* very natural till you come to the main point. Then the naturalness of all the rest makes that seem natural too; but I guess it's rather forced." Of course, like all good Howellsian readers she registers the falsity of the novel: "Why can't they let people behave reasonably in stories?" (p. 217). We expect that Penelope would object to the incredibility of the novel, but we cannot quite so easily expect her to say that in "real life" people's behavior is also irrational and incredulous. There is a curious homology developing between romance and "real life" in this logic, one that would seem not to require allegories of utopian desire to make sense. Of course, from Mencken on, Howells's critics object to his lack of concern with passion and sexuality. Penelope's unusual equation – "romance"/"real life" – could be read as reflecting just that utopian relation between women and sentimental novels that popular culture theorists discuss. In the context of this novel, however, a more specific point is being made: Romance reflects given psychological realities – no doubt socially determined around matters of gender – that dramatically present knowledge of self and others, even while the form and its reception work to deny the contradictory nature and results of that knowledge and the actions that flow from it. Tom Corey puts the matter simply, when Penelope has asked for life and fiction to be more credible: "Why shouldn't people in love behave sensibly?" (p. 217). The comic context of this remark makes the novel's point nicely. Penelope goes on to behave in just the "unnatural" way she recognizes as typical of the romance's characters. People in love behave sensibly in a logic peculiar to the stuff of desire and romance, matters neither of reason nor common sense.

The traditions of Mr. Sewell and Mrs. Lapham (as well, we must think, of some of Howells's critics) do indeed keep Penelope and Tom from seeing the lesson a novel, a romance can teach, as it catches precisely on the nature of being in love, a matter that is natural in immediacy but, on reflection, seems unnatural and irrational to boot. Of course, what is most important here is that it takes a Howellsian "realistic" novel to get beyond the immediacy of the romance, to let the "truth" of desire emerge from the forms of and the play on human – particularly, here, women's – frustrations in the business world of unfulfilled desires and repressions. The key to what Howells's novel shows, of course, is the word *natural*. The irrational characters of the romance come to a seemingly grand and heroic conclusion of self-denial and self-sacrifice. Penelope realizes the formal tricks needed to make that conclusion seem natural. Yet, of course, just what I am suggesting is that it is natural in a way neither she nor her mother nor Sewell is prepared to see; it is not sufficient as a response to a complex set of human relationships nor to the tortuous structures of human desire; but it is altogether too natural – quite precisely not commonsensical nor reasonable. In a way, we might read Penelope's success in overcoming the natural limits of romance as a victory over the natural in its immature immediacy. She does not begin from the clichéd commonsense positions of her mother and Sewell, nor does she end in them. She passes through and understands the nature and pain of irrational desire, its contradictions, its destructive drives, its procreative possibilities. She endures the Coreys and can cry for happiness and relief that finally she shall have Tom all to herself (p. 361). When Tom and Penelope finally come to speak directly, without the intrusive "manners and customs" that, as the narrator puts it, "go for more in life than our qualities" (p. 361), they speak of being oneself.

Speaking of the Corey family, Penelope says: "I couldn't be natural with them, and if I can't be natural with people, I'm disagreeable." "Can you be natural with me?," Tom replies (p. 357). In the light comedy of this romantic scene, Penelope comes to know herself, passing through the final confusions of her desire's struggle with her morality and common sense. And in a manner reminiscent of both Greek comedies and Shakespearean romances, Howells has us understand how socially and personally revitalizing all this self-discovery, this self-knowing, this self-revelation, this being in love can be. He conjoins a marriage ceremony and Lapham's own spiritual renewal. The spiritual, the individual, the moral, and the civil appear as extensions of each other: "Adversity had so far been his friend that it had taken from him all hope of the social success for which people crawl and truckle, and restored him, through failure and doubt and heartache, the manhood which his prosperity had so nearly stolen from him. Neither he nor his wife thought now that their daughter was marrying a Corey; they thought only that she was giving herself to the man who loved her" (p. 359). Of course, this marriage does not remake the entire world; this is not a ritual play nor even the world of Shakespeare's forests, but the world of imperial, monopolist Boston, the best comedy of which we glimpse in Bromfield Corey's belated irony: "His standpoint in regard to most matters was that of the sympathetic humorist who would be glad to have the victim of circumstance laugh with him, but was not too much vexed when the victim could not" (p. 267).

III

Donald Pease writes that "Emerson lived at a time when it was possible to believe the culture needed to remember nothing but its Revolutionary beginnings. Consequently he did not need to revive the cultural value of memory."[5] Arvin tells us that Howells forgot the old "Jacksonian illusions," but we might say that he did not entirely forget the Emersonian ones. Pease recreates a powerful figure in his reading of Emerson one that works here to picture some of the problems in Howells's novel. Like Emerson's "America," Lapham had "lost relation to the laws of nature, converting them instead into forms of self-interest."[6] Lapham must recover his whole self, his natural freedom and strength, and translate them into a source for his redemption and, in part, that of his culture. With his recovered or newly emergent self-reliance there can be and must be no compromise. Hence, he wrestles with the angel and rejects his tempter's, Rogers's, most subtle offerings. And, indeed, when Lapham gets beyond the point of Persis's learned and prideful Puritanism, degraded in modern Boston, it is on the basis of his own self-recovered natural strength. In a sense, then, Howells's is an Emersonian novel about possession of the power of "nature" as a shibboleth and a charm: "He could not help admiring Rogers for his ingenuity, and every selfish interest of his nature joined with many obvious duties to urge him to consent. He did not see why he should stand refuse. There was no longer a reason. He was standing out alone for nothing, any one else would say" (p. 330). Lapham's hard won self-reliance, his recovery or discovery of his natural strengths and rights become for him — indeed, he thinks these things provide the motives for his actions — they become for him social, political, and not merely personal moral forms of manners and behavior. His strength lets him look out for the interests of others. It is this transformation in Lapham that Rogers cannot fathom:

> "Why are you so particular? When you drove me out of the business you were not so very particular." Lapham winced. It was certainly ridiculous for a man who had once so selfishly consulted his own interests to be stickling now about the rights of others. (p. 330)

Howells's Lapham is, in this, an Emersonian hero, as Pease has it.

Yet, when Lapham returns to Lapham, to the past, to the natural, to the country, to self-sufficiency he becomes something of a comic figure: "Sewell was immensely interested in the moral spectacle which Lapham presented under his changed conditions. The Colonel, who was more the Colonel in those hills than he could ever have been on the Back Bay . . " (p. 363). The self-reliant Lapham, we recall, cannot even at the novel's end be certain of the motives of his acts, of their consequences, nor of what we might call their transpersonal values. He is unreflective; or, better, he reflects but cannot understand anything except the essential fact that he would ruin himself and his family again rather than wrong the interests of another.

And where does this leave the reader? As Henry Adams tells us, only a critical reader would understand how difficult it would be for Howells to pull off his feat. Surely this must mean that an attentive reader would see how Howells has constructed his novel so that the readers would see themselves — as Howells's text self-evidently shows itself to be — thoroughly implicated in all of the games played with the various forms of cultural reserve which stand, as Heidegger might put it, ready to be drawn on by the productive forces — and that includes the critical, artistic forces of a business society.[7]

41

IV

We began with Arvin's and went on to James's varying comments on Howells's value in American culture. It is to the thought about culture and the criticism of culture to which they lead that we should now return. Howells's novel, I think, shows itself to be too immanent to the culture it presumably critiques for it to allow itself to be seen as an adequate fulcrum upon which it might be possible to model a critique of U.S. culture. In fact, in its very immanence to U.S. culture, it marks the limits, as it were, to the value of immanental critique. Howells's novel works, in so far as it does, because it can assuredly draw upon certain psychoaesthetic, certain sociocultural, certain ideological formations within U.S. society and its readily available cultural memories. We have called some of these romance, democracy, common sense, and natural man. Newton Arvin celebrates Howells precisely for using the readily available and, one must presume, politically still important and valuable cultural resources of liberal America to celebrate its own abilities to reform, better itself, and perdure.

But what lesson is there for criticism in this situation? First, it reminds us of what inevitably happens to the liberal or bourgeois mind when it necessarily becomes part of an increasingly socialized culture. That mind loses the necessary distinction that could have allowed it the free exercise that might have been possible when culture still stood in some forceful opposition to society and politics. The loss of that distinction – a loss marked in Howells's novel by the circulation of romances among women and the shaded figure of Bromfield Corey – means the absorption of the critical mind into the sociocultural apparatus that is the obvious and apparent object of critique. Taking seriously Arvin's perception that Howells portrayed the new forms of capitalism emergent in the United States after the Civil War means taking seriously as well the traces (some of which I have remarked) that delimit the critical mind – including Howells's own realistic one – in its operations upon its objects.

Second, it lets us think about the gentle ironies of Adams's remarks about Howells's skills. All of Howells's work is sleight-of-hand and only a "critical reader" will see how hard it is not to fail at such an effort. No one more than Adams knew the changes occurring in the United States after the Civil War. No one more than Adams measured the historical drift from the Revolutionary ideology and social forms. No one more than Adams, even in 1872, knew more about the current postwar debates about the nature and origins of American democracy. Only Henry James knew as much about the startling thinness of U.S. culture. A critical reader sees that Howells's effort *is* sleight-of-hand; it is a thin trick playing out the shallow vein of what James called "the small and the vulgar." A critical reader can at most applaud the magician's success in trying such risky tricks; the mortification that follows upon the magician's failure is not, in this case, merely embarrassment, but the discovery of the reality that the delusion has masked for a time in its very daring games with the familiar, the ordinary, the commonplace – games played with the culture's population, with the audience that is the reservoir of memory, ideology, psychic response, and common sense – all those things that make up the text of *The Rise of Silas Lapham.*

But if the extension of socialization throughout culture includes the critical artistic mind, and the critical journalistic mind if we judge by Arvin, then what is left for the American critic of U.S. culture? Of course, we have seen any number of efforts to deal with the problem facing critical intellectuals practicing critiques upon their own cultures, and we have seen that, for the most part, when they have reflected upon the difficulties posed by this specular position they extend themselves into the study of their own minds and their products as if such study will somehow yield up insight into the proper tactics for such enmeshed minds. Critics call this the double bind, or duplicity, or irony, or suspicion, or, most recently, ethnography.[8] Adorno puts the matter of the fate of criticism this way: "It pursues the logics of its aporias, the insolubility of the task itself."[9] As the work of Althusser and Macherey suggests, such criticism thinks itself successful when it can identify the unresolved contradictions of society and perhaps even propose more scientific resolutions of those contradictions. Indeed, I have looked at Howells's novel to suggest that it ends with only a "spurious harmony,"[10] a false response to the disharmonies Arvin credits Howells with perceiving. But I am also suggesting that criticism of U.S. society, like that carried out by Howells and Arvin, typically can offer nothing more than an idea of harmony inversely suggested by the inharmonious resolution apparent to Adams's "critical reader." Cultural criticism, in this mode, in the United States, can do little more than itself carry all the marks of the contradictions it describes or dramatizes and no more than extend the replication of the society that depends upon its ruling ideologies to renew itself free of meaningful challenge to its hegemony. Adorno would have it that in such a world even to speak of "ideology" in the classical sense as "false consciousness" – even, I would add, to think of it in Althusserian terms[11] – is both absurd and redundant: "There are no more ideologies in the authentic sense of false consciousness, only advertisements for the world through its duplication and the provocative lie which does not seek belief but commands silence."[12] *The Rise of Silas Lapham* does not redeem society as Arvin's criticism suggests. No artistic, cultural, critical object or effort can do when socialization extends itself to the point that its reserves are omnipresent, if not always recognized, and essentially available in their form as advertisements for the society even when made over by the critical mind – immanent to those reserves – into critique. "Even the most radical reflection of the mind on its own failure is limited by the fact that it remains only reflection, without altering the existence to which its failure bears witness."[13] Of course, critics have often called Adorno to task for not realizing how fully this insight pertains to his own position, even when he calls for dialectics: "The dialectical critic of culture must both participate in culture and not participate."[14] But glossing Adorno and Howells this way does not deny the problem. Both give us a very strong sense of the position of criticism within the modernized reifications of U.S. society. Given that unavoidable position "within," the liberal line found in Arvin, even its ironic perversion in Adams and James, seems most acceptable because it is most available and most approved. The critical realism of Howells does double duty for the culture it critiques; this is not the infamous "double bind" that worries some weak critics. Rather it is an acknowledgment of the facts of all criticism carried out imminently, carried out too close to the terms and values of the United States. Perhaps it is an acknowledgment of some of the inherent sociocultural and political problems of the study of American culture itself.

NOTES

1. Newton Arvin, "The Usableness of Howells," *The New Republic* 91 (June 30, 1937): 227.
2. On this matter, see the definitive work by Donald Pease, *Visionary Compacts: American Renaissance Writings in Cultural Context* (Madison: University of Wisconsin Press, 1987), esp. pp. 7–24.
3. Henry James, "William Dean Howells," *Harper's Weekly* (June 19, 1886), 394–5.
4. William Dean Howells, *The Rise of Silas Lapham* (New York: Viking Penguin, 1983), p. 102; *Silas Lapham* is hereafter referred to by page number in the text.
5. Pease, *Visionary Compacts*, p. 213.
6. Ibid., p. 214.
7. I'm thinking here, of course, of Heidegger's difficult text, "The Question Concerning Technology," in *The Question Concerning Technology and Other Essays*, trans. William Lovitt (New York: Harper & Row, 1977), p. 16.
8. James Clifford, *The Predicament of Culture: Twentieth-Century Ethnography, Literature, and Art* (Cambridge, Mass.: Harvard University Press, 1988).
9. Theodor Adorno, "Cultural Criticism and Society," *Prisms*, trans. Samuel Weber (Cambridge, Mass.: MIT Press, 1981), p. 32.
10. Ibid.
11. See Louis Althusser, "Ideology and Ideological State Apparatuses," in *Lenin and Philosophy*, trans. Ben Brewster (London: NLB, 1971), pp. 120–73.
12. Adorno, *Prisms*, p. 34.
13. Ibid., p. 33.
14. Ibid.

The Hole in Howells / The Lapse in *Silas Lapham*

JOHN SEELYE

L IKE houses, novels have proper entranceways intended by the author as the way into the fiction that follows, and like an architect, the author designs those licensed openings for maximum aesthetic effect, so as to lure us into the narrative structure beyond. That linear interior is likewise an arrangement laid out so as to enhance the experience of encounter, and it subjoins the entranceway as a complex instrument of authorial control. Entering a novel by means of the first word, sentence, chapter, and proceeding along the intended corridor is a convention basic to the act of fiction, but it is a route like that found in a carefully planned theme park, managed by the controlling intelligence so as to exercise full aesthetic authority. But should the reader get into the narrative by another, unintended opening, then quite a different route is followed and a different experience may be obtained, one controlled not by the author-architect but by the reader as explorer of forbidden spaces.

The kind of opening I am describing provides access not to the narrative but to the workings of the narrative, the infrastructure that lies within the story by means of which the author leads us. Moreover, by gaining access to the infrastructure, by discovering the way the novel has been designed to work, we can often gain access to the author as well. *The Rise of Silas Lapham* provides a convenient (but by no means unique) example, for we know that the writing of this novel coincided with something close to a nervous breakdown experienced by Howells, that its carefully worked out social drama seems to have put a great strain on the author in order to bring it to a satisfactory conclusion.[1]

That strain I would suggest is responsible for a major flaw in the novel at precisely the point where psychological motivation needs to be entirely credible but is not, the episode in which Tom Corey, having recoiled from Lapham's outcry of naked shame, following the disastrous dinner party, determines to ask for Penelope's hand in marriage. This flaw, with its notable lapse in the decorum of literary realism, provides just such an opening as I have earlier described, by which we can enter the infrastructure of the novel and even penetrate beyond into the consciousness of the author. But before demonstrating that possibility, I should like to turn to the other opening, the one intended by Howells as the main entrance to his novel, which was designed to serve not only as an instrument of aesthetic control but as a carefully phrased preparation for the incident that precedes the critical confrontation between Silas Lapham and his young employee.

The first chapter of *Silas Lapham* has been justly praised as a tour de force by means of which Howells introduces his main character and provides a masterful résumé of his personality and origins. As such, it is a quiet equivalent to that corresponding but much more dramatic episode, the Corey dinner party, during which Howells has his character demonstrate his social inadequacies, thereby dooming himself to the consequences of those personal qualities so trenchantly outlined at the start of the novel. By means of the interview conducted by Bartley Hubbard, a journalist who had figured prominently in an earlier novel, *A Modern Instance*, Howells was able to provide considerable material suitably condensed, including a detailed physical description of Lapham (set down by Hubbard in his notebook) and the newly made millionaire's life story (narrated by him at Hubbard's request). Not only was Howells thereby able to furnish details necessary for the novel's development without resorting to authorial comment and synopses – anathema to the "realistic" writer – but he was able to give ironic point to the introduction of his main character by means of the newsman's condescending attitude toward his subject. Hubbard is a confidence man of sorts, professing a genuine interest in whomever he is interviewing, letting his subjects ramble on innocently, until they have provided him with sufficient material to make fools of them in the printed story. A writer himself, he is a substitute for the authorial presence, and though hardly to be taken as a spokesman for Howells, he carries out some necessary dirty work at the start.

By these means, Howells provides a complex statement of the facts of Lapham's early life and career, so that we are left with a divided view of the paint manufacturer, whose bluff, sincere, plainspoken manner can, if encouraged, swell into self-congratulation and boasting. In the end, Hubbard's wife Marcia is so pleased with the gift of paint sent her by Lapham that she pleads with her husband not to "make fun of him, as you do some of those people," earning Hubbard's assurance that whatever he does to Lapham in the published interview, it will be "nothing that *he'll* ever find out" (p. 23). We are led to understand that not all of Boston is as impressed as Lapham is with his achievement. For Hubbard, he is simply "the old fool . . . the mineral paint man," who has had the temerity to advertise his product by painting advertisements on the native rocks of New England.

And yet, as Bartley's bride insists, Lapham is "a good man," justly proud of his paint, his success, his own wife. At an early moment in the interview, Hubbard somewhat overreaches himself by a series of self-mocking questions: "Any barefoot business? Early deprivations of any kind, that would encourage the youthful reader to go and do likewise?" To this Lapham delivers a gentle rebuff, having "looked at him silently, and then said with quiet self-respect, 'I guess if you see these things as a joke, my life wont inter*est* you'" (p. 5). Hubbard reassures him and "beguiles" Silas into continuing with the interview, but the moment is decisive. We see that Lapham is not quite the "old fool" Hubbard calls him; we also see that Bartley is hardly an unqualified spokesman for the author, but rather is being set up to reveal as much about himself as about the subject of his interview.

Moreover, the readers familiar with *A Modern Instance* are provided with a complex perspective within which to set the first chapter of *Silas Lapham*. For there Hubbard is shown to be a ruthlessly ambitious journalist who will stop at nothing in his quest for success, an amoral creation of the "modern times" of which he is so flagrant an "instance." Having been shot dead by a victim of his slandering journalism at the close of the novel in

49

which he first figures, Bartley Hubbard is at the start of *Silas Lapham* a ghostly apparition, whose presence lends a foreboding note to the opening episode of the novel that follows. His eventual fate gives a grim cast to the conversation Hubbard has with his wife that evening, as he rails at the "limitations of decency" that keep him from printing "just what Colonel Lapham thought of landscape advertising in Colonel Lapham's own words" (p. 21) (Lapham had said that "the landscape was made for man, and not man for the landscape. . . . I never saw anything so very sacred about a big rock, along a river or in a pasture that it wouldn't do to put mineral paint on it in three colors," pp. 14–15). This penchant of Lapham's for advertising his paint across the face of the countryside will be one of several qualities that offend his future brother-in-law, the aesthete Bromfield Corey, and would have been equally offensive to Howells or any sensitive reader of the day. Yet Hubbard is about to discover the package of paint sent to his wife, a gesture emanating from Lapham's natural vein of generosity.

First, however, he brings up a subject that Howells has left unmentioned to that point, one that is tangential to Hubbard's own personal failings: "I'll tell you one thing," he says to his wife, intending to tease her, "he had a girl there at one of the desks that you wouldn't let *me* have within gunshot of *my* office. Pretty? It ain't any name for it!" (p. 21). This remark is a critical jointure between the two novels, occurring at a moment in the lives of Bartley and Marcia when they have recently reconciled (and married) after a long separation occasioned by Bartley's presumed philanderings during their engagement. The remark seems chiefly a callous signal alluding to his unsavory character (developed fully in *Modern Instance*) and might be passed by without much thought, but its interjection at this moment, between his snorting at Lapham's notion of the proper uses of the landscape and his opening the gift of paint, is a superb bit of dramatic irony. Not only does it (like the remark about the "limits of decency") look forward in terms of the fictional time frame to events that will happen in *A Modern Instance* as well as to events that have already occurred in that book, but the beautiful girl herself, hitherto not mentioned, is going to be the subject of considerable conjecture and eventual revelation during the unfolding action of *Silas Lapham*. To have

Bartley, himself associated with philandering (and its consequences), be the first to remark on the girl's anomalous presence in Lapham's office, plants a carefully nurtured seed of associative guilt that will first shadow Lapham's character and then, when removed, give it added luster.

This is the kind of craftsmanship we can attribute to a writer firmly in control of his art – and his reader – and it may be compared to the interview between Lapham and Tom Corey that eventually results in the revelation of Tom's true love interest. For there Howells does not seem to be in firm command of his narrative, as defined by motivation. Setting aside for the moment Tom Corey's rapid shifts of attitude, we can concentrate on Lapham's sudden and total self-abasement to a much younger man with whom he has previously maintained a carefully controlled, relatively distant and formal relationship. Where we can accept Silas's boasting during a dinner party as a habit of long standing, his initial reserve dissipated by his unaccustomed consumption of alcohol, what can we say about this sudden lowering of himself in a terribly mistaken attempt to make amends, coming as it does from a man carefully defined for us as extremely sensitive to matters of personal honor? Lapham, we have earlier been told, "had the pride which comes of self-making, and he would not openly lower his crest to the young fellow he had taken into his business" (p. 108). This would seem to be a decided lapse in the decorum of realism, so carefully and ingeniously maintained in the opening chapter.

What, then, can we make of this staggeringly inappropriate and uncharacteristic gesture? Why did Howells set up a scene so embarrassing to young Corey as to arouse shock and disgust, an expression of "his own allegiance to the exclusiveness to which he was born and bred, as a man perceives his duty to his country when her rights are invaded," necessitating the sudden reversal, a scant two pages later, when Corey experiences a "mood, romantic and exalted," toward his employer, a reversal that is, if anything, less believable than Lapham's lapse in self-control (pp. 211, 213)? There is nothing in Tom's initial reaction that cannot be reconciled to predictable patterns of behavior; nor have we been entirely unprepared for Corey's quick turnabout, once he has fled the office and his employer, during which he struggles to master his loathing by attempting to see matters from Lapham's viewpoint. But when Tom suddenly resolves to make amends for his hostile reaction by asking Silas for Penelope's hand in marriage, we are forced to wonder if the act is "realistic" or an absolute surrender to the exigencies of plot, a surrender made even more abject by subjoining it to Silas's own uncharacteristic outburst. Would a sensitive young man, most particularly of Corey's social background, make such a dramatic turnabout, from reviling Lapham for his boorish insensitivity, to rushing to his home in order to make known his feelings for Penelope?

This is an extremely important moment, virtually the climax of the novel, not only because it marks the start of Silas's decline and fall – the major theme and action in the story – but because it inspires Tom Corey to take a step equally strategic to the generic lines of the plot. Since everyone in the novel (and not a few readers) have assumed to this point that Tom is in love with the "other" sister, Irene, any such declaration is bound to be a difficult matter to arrange within the conventions of realistic fiction, most especially since the situation of the mistaken lover is a device familiar to romantic and sentimental modes. To set it in sequence with a dual lapse in characteristic behavior is to call more attention to it than an author in control of character and event would wish to elicit. We can accept Corey's embarrassment in the face of his employer's confession and plea and we can accept the young man's preference for Penelope over Irene, even his decision to marry the older, less pretty but far more intelligent daughter. But that he should choose this particular moment to wed not only Lapham's daughter but necessarily the two families, whose differences have been made suddenly and glaringly obvious, is very difficult to accept. It is, however, for our present purposes a beneficial lapse, providing a sudden opening in the architectonics of the story through which we may enter the infrastructure.

For the marriage of Tom and Penelope is absolutely essential to the working out of the novel within the framework of Howells's subtextual argument about literary realism. That is, Corey's declaration signals the start of the action that Howells intended as a definition of "realism" in terms of ethical and moral choice within the parameters of formulaic fiction. As such, it is entirely a "literary" signal, the start of a sequence that foregrounds the fiction-as-fiction aspects of the book, making it a self-illustrating creative act. Howells's spokesman here is the Reverend Sewell, whose attack on sentimental novels clearly expresses the author's own feelings, and the specific text under attack, a novel titled "Tears, Idle Tears," is the very book that Penelope Lapham has been reading and that she commonsensically dismisses as "silly," only to find herself later emulating the self-sacrificing denial of the "old-fashioned" heroine by insisting against all reason that she and Tom "must suffer" by denying their love (pp. 217, 256). In the end, Penelope obeys the dictates of reason (and realistic fiction), aided by the encouragement of her parents (who have been bolstered by the commonsensical Sewell), and elects after a period of emotional anguish to accept Tom's proposal, the suffering of her sister having been determined by all parties (including Irene) as unavoidable. She elects that is a "realistic" as opposed to a "romantic" (or sentimental) course of action. The last third of the book therefore serves to illustrate Howells's doctrine concerning the harmfulness of sentimental fiction by posing in a realistic fiction an alternative solution. The result, however, constantly calls the attention of the reader to the hyperliterariness of the fictive occasion, converting a romantic plot device (the mistaken lover) to the ends of realistic fiction.

Of course, it can be (and has been) said that realistic fiction in general has a Bloomian rationale, obeying a dialectic traceable to the Cervantesean necessity of assuming sentimental postures in order to trip them up. "Realism," finally, is antisentimentalism, most particularly as practiced by Howells and Twain. But this does not explain away Howells's apparently perverse decision to trigger the terms of this ideological dialectic by means of Lapham's uncharacteristic apology and Corey's unlikely reversal. Could we not imagine alternative behavior, permitting more believable reactions? Could there not have been an interview with Corey that maintains distance and dignity, awakening in the young man a deepening of sympathy and understanding for his troubled employer, so that we could accede to his sudden resolve "to see Lapham and give him an ultimate proof of his own perfect faith and unabated respect" (p. 213)? We have earlier been told that Corey is able to subordinate himself to a man who is clearly his social and intellectual inferior because of "the sense of discipline which is innate in the apparently insubordinate American nature," and only an equivalent display of control (of which Lapham is quite capable) could possibly arouse in Corey such an otherwise quixotic response as conceiving of marriage as "reparation" (p. 110).

A skillful writer, Howells by and large is successful in matters of plot engineering, and the lapse to which I have been referring seems not to have bothered most readers. Moreover, he is also so accomplished in his presentation of character and motive in general that he seems to have convinced readers for more than a century that Silas and his wife deserve the sentence of perpetual rustication with which the novel ends, that no other resolution is possible. Yet in his handling of the marriage of Tom and Penelope, Howells demonstrates that social impasses may be solved by a fictional version of statist compromise, sending the newlyweds off to Mexico for a cooling-off period, then (apparently) bringing them back to Boston, convenient turns of plot promoting the desirable end of unity through resolution. Surely something similar could have been arranged for Silas and his wife, something, that is, short of total ruin and permanent exile to Vermont. While acknowledging that in order to "rise," Silas must fall, why, we should wonder, is his punishment so complete. Indeed why is he punished at all?

We can in part answer that question by considering the nature of the crime for which he is being punished, which is not so much his earlier sin against his partner, Milton Rogers, as the pride that inspires him to attempt connections with his social and intellectual superiors, the sort of hubris that is involved in the fall of tragic figures, like King Lear, whom Silas somewhat resembles. Lear, having been so blinded by pride as to think he can keep the prerogatives of power without its responsibilities, is stripped of his retainers, loses his favorite daughter, goes mad, and dies of a broken heart. Silas, so vain as to think he can be accepted as an equal by "Society" because of his wealth, loses his fortune, his house, and worst of all the paint company he has built. He saves his sanity and does not die, but he ends a broken, humbled man, who accepts his punishment as just, even though his ruin was brought about finally not by his faults but because he was unwilling to defraud another, hardly a character flaw, but rather a sign of moral strength.

Howells, once again, is successful in convincing us that what happens *must* happen, that Silas moreover is the central figure in a morality play not a tragedy. And yet the temptation to which his hero yields would seem to have little relevance to any conventional moral scheme, but rather has reference to what we might call the Boston "scheme of things," which the action of the novel validates. What Howells has really convinced us of is that Silas and Persis Lapham do not "fit," that they must therefore be expelled from polite society, an expulsion made even more secure by removing them not only from Boston but from Massachusetts. "Society," opines Bromfield Corey, "is a very different sort of thing from good sense and right ideas. It is based upon them, of course, but the airy, graceful, winning superstructure which we all know demands different qualities" (p. 138). What Bromfield is talking about is what he so amply illustrates, which is good taste, to which matters of moral perfection are not relevant, no more than the statues of "Faith" and "Prayer" redeem the tastelessness of the Lapham parlor but rather enforce it.[2]

To understand this is to comprehend the subtextual implication of the Reverend Sewell's insistence that "the commonplace" is the most suitable material for realistic fiction. For Silas's sin is that he is entirely too commonplace to qualify for admission to Boston society, even though that exclusive, self-defining community has always managed to find room for the newest of the new wealthy who aspire to join its exclusive ranks. As if to prove the point, the Bromfield Coreys, even after the Colonel's disgrace at their dinner party, continue reluctantly to accept the necessity of making their peace with the Laphams for the sake of their son's happiness. It is not they who determine that Silas and his family must leave Boston, but "fate," the workings of which are controlled by the author, and which certify that the Laphams lack the social grace necessary for election to that "airy, graceful, winning superstructure" that is the Bostonian secular Heaven. It is not, finally, Silas's behavior at the dinner party that condemns him, but his complete breakdown before Tom Corey. It is that confession of shame that drives home the final wedge, not so much between the Laphams and the Coreys, or even between Silas and Tom, as between Silas and ourselves, for now we understand completely and absolutely that the paint manufacturer, even sober, does not understand correct behavior, having breached the kind of social decorum that is to tastefulness closely allied. The "commonplace" that Howells finally asserts is his alone to enforce, that common place in the social order to which he returns his overly ambitious manufacturer and his confused, unhappy wife.

Howells was willing to salvage the love affair between Tom and Penelope, promoting the marriage essential to the novel of manners (and popular fiction), but only by undercutting it with unlikely turns of plot and character motivation – the same devices that engineer Silas's destruction. He then bundled the couple off in a cloud of authorial convenience previously provided for – Tom's knowledge of Spanish and the long-deferred plans for expanding paint sales into South America – in effect discounting its relevance to the basic situation and thereby leaving the social division intact. As a "moral action," therefore, the novel has a carefully programmed dénouement in which all of the major characters are led to make decisions or take actions that do not challenge the established order but enforce it. Chief of these is the decision by the titular hero to sacrifice his fortune and his factory in order to satisfy the urgings of conscience, a situation carefully rigged so that while we admire Silas for his sterling morality we are not led to condemn the system that brought about this dilemma. Where Howells was willing to argue that self-sacrifice is wrong in affairs of the heart, being equated with sentimentality, he convinces us that in matters of social and business arrangements it seems to be still a fictive necessity. He leaves us convinced that Silas could only have done what he did – that there was no alternative choice – that the sacrifice was as inevitable as Christ's. He thereby surrounded the sacred precincts of Boston with the sort of providential iron wall that John Winthrop had sought to erect but to different ends.

Again, the turning point occurs during the painful interview between Silas Lapham and Tom Corey, the demonstration of a social flaw that, while determining the subsequent action, also opens up the fabric of the text. Thus Lapham's lapse is also Howells's, and if it is Silas's fatal slip that sends him Faustus-like down the chute to social exile, then we should further consider the implications of that inglorious hole to our understanding of Howells's own psychological fabric. If entering that opportune opening allows us to explore the structural implications of Howells's "moral" action, then we need to move deeper into the consciousness of the man who determined the social agenda that the infrastructure illustrates. For though it has been generally understood that the nervous breakdown Howells suffered while writing *Silas Lapham* seems to have been brought on by his forcible confrontation, both in the novel and all about him, with glaring discrepancies in American life that his psychic stuff was too weak to contain, no one has taken the next and presumably necessary step, demonstrating that the novel likewise failed in similar fashion. That is, if Howells found "the bottom falling out" of his received sense of social status, perhaps it was because he was attempting to structure in fiction the sort of compromise he had himself managed to maintain between his own deep democratic faith and the aristocratic values of his adopted Boston. The equilibrist suddenly found the tightrope disappearing beneath him, and hastened to the safety of aristos and the consolations of good taste, leaving Lapham to fall upward into Vermont.

The poles between which that rope had been stretched may be figured as Mark Twain and Henry James. That Howells had been able to maintain parallel friendships and correspondence with both men most certainly demonstrates remarkable powers of personal and artistic balance. The implications of the loss of artistic balance in *Silas Lapham* to Howells's personal dilemma are better understood, moreover, by enumerating the similarities between the hero of that novel and Mark Twain, which are extensive, including the red hair, rural origins, daughter-and-wife-ridden domestic lives, the building of expensive, architect-designed homes (Clemens's house in Hartford was going up as *Silas Lapham* was being written), social unease in high Boston places (T. B. Aldrich's widow recalled mistaking Clemens for a drunk when her husband once brought him home for dinner unannounced and unidentified), and, most important, success built upon the clever marketing of a "natural" gift, whether figured as a paint mine or a deep, rich vein of humor, literally discovered by Clemens in the mining country of Nevada.[3]

"Silas," after all, means "man of the woods," evoking that orangutan image that Mark Twain elicited, with his wild head of red hair, luxuriant moustaches, and unpredictable behavior tending toward theatrical display. Even "Lapham" alternatively pronounced suggests laughter, and the paint manufacturer declares his preference for popular stage comedy, including "Sellers," the dramatized version of *The Gilded Age* that took its title from the Micawberish "Colonel" who figures prominently in the play and the book, a connection made firmer by the title that "Colonel Lapham" also enjoys. At an early point in the novel Penelope Lapham (who has a humorous "drawl" like Clemens's and an infectious chuckle) drops a reference to Twain's famous story about a bullfrog, as her sister, who has inherited the father's red hair, collapses in helpless laughter. Like Clemens also, Silas Lapham (whose name contains the humorist's first two initials) has a tender conscience combined with a paranoid business style; the label on his jars of paint advertises the date on which his father discovered the paint mine, 1835, Clemens's date of birth, and 1855, when the son first marketed it, a convenient enough date for the emergence of Clemens's literary talents.[4]

But the most telling link between the events in Howells's novel and Mark Twain's life is established by the parallels, enumerated by Kermit Vanderbilt, between the dinner party in *Silas Lapham* and the infamous Whittier Birthday Celebration of 1877, during which Twain had delivered a speech that both he and Howells immediately recognized as a monstrous social gaffe. The incident has been fully explored by Henry Nash Smith for its relevance to the uneasiness Clemens felt while moving among Brahmins, and Kenneth Lynn has likewise pointed to the episode as reflecting Howells's sense of being an "imposter" in Boston.[5] Notably, Howells dismissed the speech as "that hideous mistake of poor Clemens's," distancing himself from his friend even while commiserating with him. For like Lapham, Clemens went through embarrassing contortions of apology – the chief writhings of which bear close resemblance to Lapham's – first to Howells, and then, mistaking a hint from his friend, in a lengthy letter to the presumed offended parties, a letter that Lynn assumes was regarded by Howells with favor: "In the short run, then, Howells was glad that Twain had been willing to go down on his knees, so to speak, and beg for mercy. But how glad was he in the long run, as he quietly reviewed the matter in his mind in the years after 1877? We can never know for sure, inasmuch as Howells has left us no record of his thoughts."[6] To the contrary, I think that Howells must have been if anything more discomfited by Twain's letter than by his apology to himself. More important, in Tom Corey's horrified reaction to Lapham's abject self-debasement, I think we have a reasonable facsimile of Howells's own dismay when confronted by a social lapse even more distressing to him than the mistaken speech itself.

This is not to say that we should regard Tom Corey as an autobiographical projection, yet there are aspects of the young man who is described as being rescued from "being commonplace . . . through some combination of qualities of the heart that made men trust him . . . [that] women call . . . sweet" that place him in a curiously equilibrist position (p. 127). There is a carefully mounted contrast between the young man's social conditioning and place and his sudden decision to "go into paint," a turnabout attributed to Tom's physical resemblance to his paternal grandfather, a well-known Boston merchant. While resembling his grandfather in his aquiline nose, Tom we are told lacks the "predatory fierceness" of the old India merchant, having "the Roman nose and the energy" but an added quality of "gentleness" (pp. 70–1). Corey is something of a genetic throwback, a cultivated scion of a Brahmin aesthete who, thanks to his heritage, can vibrate sympathetically to what his father calls "the romance, the poetry of our age" — making money (p. 64).

He is a bridge therefore between his father and the man he works for, and if Lapham resembles in many specifics Samuel L. Clemens, then Bromfield Corey, in general terms, is an equivalent Henry James, Jr. Both men are enabled to enjoy lives dedicated to art and good taste because of the labors of their progenitors, in James's case his grandfather, the prominent Albany merchant William James. In Lapham's view, Bromfield Corey "had spent his youth abroad and his father's money everywhere, and done nothing but say smart things" (p. 92). To the contrary, Corey had gone to Europe to improve himself as a painter, much as James expatriated himself to perfect his novelist's art, but in the end he does become something of a dilettante, justifying Lapham's grumpy dismissal of him as "everything that was offensively aristocratic."

James, for his part, had in *The American* (1877) produced an equivalent type to Lapham, a newly rich manufacturer of washtubs who sets his sights on an aristocratic European woman, whom he regards at the start as the chief prize among the cultural artifacts he seeks to purchase while abroad, and at the last as an object of chivalric knight-errantry. Over the protest of Howells, who was charmed by the possibility of such a unique marriage of cultures, James drove a sharp, unyielding wedge between the two products of diverse civilizations, determining the impossibility of such a union. He came to much the same conclusion a year later in *Daisy Miller*, this time structuring a plot that holds out the possibility of a marriage between a sprightly, ingenuous, and pretty young American girl and a Europeanized American man, only to demonstrate the unlikeliness of any such union by mounting a series of misunderstandings that leads to the heroine's death.

Modern readers are apt to sympathize with Daisy, but to James's contemporaries her flirtatiousness was regarded as an early version of ugly Americanism, and is referred to as such by Bartley Hubbard in his story on Lapham. In describing Persis Lapham (whom he has not met) as "one of those women who, in whatever walk of life, seem born to honor the name of American Woman," he opposes her to "the national reproach of Daisy Millerism" (p. 21). But one of the Lapham daughters, alluded to only in passing by Hubbard, is something of a carbon copy for Daisy, for Irene also sets her heart on a man who has nothing but a passing interest in her, and while hardly a persistent flirt, she does what she can to encourage romantic overtures. She is aided in this by her mother, who like Mrs. Miller contrives to leave Irene alone with young Corey: "In her own girlhood it was supposed that if a young man seemed to be coming to see a girl, it was only common sense to suppose that he wished to see her alone," just the sort of "common sense" that results in Daisy's tragic end (p. 151).

By contrast, the marriage between Tom Corey and the "elder daughter" of the Laphams is just the sort of transcultural union Henry James regarded as impossible, but it is brought about by considerable novelistic engineering. First, there is Penelope's love of good literature and conversation, to which we must add Tom's atavistic business sense, along with that convenient three-year removal to Mexico pending the newlyweds' return. As for the possibility of eventual reunion between the Bromfield and Tom Coreys, founded on "traits in Penelope's character which finally reconciled all her husband's family and endeared her to them," Howells notes wryly that "these things continually happen in novels; and the Coreys, as they had always promised themselves to do, made the best, and not the worst, of Tom's marriage," an interesting pairing that is less a resolution than a final forestalling (p. 359).

What we have in *Silas Lapham*, after all, is supposed to be a novel that avoids those kinds of convenient novelistic resolutions. As we have already seen, moreover, Tom Corey's decision to marry Penelope is a superliterary moment, intimately connected with glaring evidence of the Laphams' unsuitableness for Boston society. We come much closer I think to Howells's true conclusion in his later authorial pronouncement concerning the "manners and customs" that "go for more in life than our qualities," for it is manners and customs finally that place an unbridgeable gap between the Laphams and the Coreys:

> The price that we pay for civilization is the fine yet impassable differentiation of these. Perhaps we pay too much; but it will not be possible to persuade those who have the difference in their favor that this is so. They may be right; and at any rate the blank misgiving, the recurring sense of disappointment to which the young people's departure [for Mexico] left the Coreys is to be considered. That was the end of their son and brother for them; they felt that; and they were not mean or unamiable people. (p. 361)

In the end, then, Howells took a position not much different from James's, leaving the newlyweds in a kind of social limbo, much as he had sent Silas and his wife off to Vermont.[7]

If the Jamesian Coreys seem reconciled to the loss of their son as a necessary concomitant to keeping his bride at a distance, their grief is further assuaged by the removal of her Twainsian parents from Boston. This happy circumstance is attributed to "a higher power," presumably as a reward for their "good intentions" to accept the Laphams into their circle as part of the regrettable necessity of accepting Tom's marriage: "This marriage had not, thanks to an overruling Providence, brought the succession of Lapham teas upon Bromfield Corey which he had dreaded" (p. 360). But the "overruling Providence" in a novel is the author, and it was Howells, as we have determined earlier, who was responsible for removing the Laphams to "their native fastnesses," alleviating the horrible necessity of entertaining them at tea. Such things also "continually happen in novels," and as for Bromfield Corey's continuing attitude toward his son's uncouth father-in-law, distance permitted "a delicate, aesthetic pleasure in the heroism with which Lapham had withstood Rogers and his temptations – something finely dramatic and unconsciously effective," something, that is, not unlike what happens in *Silas Lapham* (p. 359). We cannot discount a certain fine irony here, for Bromfield is clearly intended by Howells for a snob, but neither can we overlook the ideological implications of distancing human agony by means of a frame, which is precisely what Howells does to solve the aesthetic problem of Silas Lapham.

We can further reinforce this point by referring to the Reverend Sewell, whose Howellsian advice is so important to the working out of the subtextual elements, for he "was immensely interested" likewise "in the *moral spectacle* that Lapham presented under his changed conditions" (p. 363, emphasis added). It is Sewell's visit to Vermont to savor the spectacle closely that gives us our last glimpse of the humbled paint manufacturer, reconciled to the fitness of his response to the moral question presented to him in the deal arranged by his private devil, Milton Rogers. Asked by Sewell whether he has any regrets for having refused the opportunity to recoup his fortune by "selling out to those Englishmen," Lapham resorts to a curious turn of phrase: "Well, it don't always seem if I done it. . . . Seems sometimes as if it was *a hole opened for me*, and I crept out of it. . . . I don't know as I should always say it paid; but if I done it, and the thing was to do over again, right in the same way, I guess I should have to do it" (p. 365, emphasis added).

The notion of a hole divinely opened so as to provide a providential guide is an old Puritan notion, completely in keeping with that conception of the New England conscience that the character of Silas Lapham illustrates. But in terms of the structure of the novel itself, it evokes also the hole through which Howells found himself falling in 1884. It was that hole that resulted in the opening through which we have obtained access to the book's infrastructure, exploring the implications of Lapham's outcry of shame and Tom Corey's unlikely reaction to it. Where Silas's outcry warrants his fall and expulsion, Corey's reaction results in a union that Howells could permit only by arranging a "providential" hole through which the Bromfield Coreys could escape. In the end, he effected just the kind of stalemated separation so characteristic of a Jamesian novel, but by so doing he violated that part of him that was attracted to Mark Twain.

Howells's own dilemma regarding Twain was less moral than social, and where he was in person able to perform a marvelously adroit balancing act by maintaining a dual friendship with Clemens and Henry James, it necessitated keeping his two friends far apart. Only in him were they united, a unity that demonstrated Howells's own deep division, that imperfectly joined filamentation that held him suspended over the immense gulf separating paint manufacturers and Western humorists from the aristocrats and aesthetes of Boston. In *Silas Lapham* he held out the possibility of a union between these unreconcilable parts only to dismiss that likelihood by arranging events in such a way as to enforce social barriers, relying on the social gaffe of his friend Mark Twain and its painful consequences as justification. The memory of Twain's violation of Boston decorum brought Howells face to face with the impossibility of certain unions except "in novels," and as if to demonstrate the difficulty of mounting such a union in a "realistic" novel, he effected the dénouement of *Silas Lapham* by stretching the fabric of *vraisemblance* to the tearing point. Finally, Howells emphasized the unlikeliness of the Corey–Lapham union by hinging it to an impossible motive, Tom's sudden resolve to rectify his flight from Lapham by marrying his daughter.

In the end, Howells's "nature's nobleman" (as Bartley Hubbard calls him) is put where he belongs – back in nature. In the end, Bromfield Corey can accept Lapham only as a species of Noble

Savage, an aesthetic even a romantic figure in a moral landscape set side by side with the portrait he has painted of his father, the Silas Lapham of an earlier era. And this is precisely what Howells himself has done in this novel with the man he called "My Mark Twain." In effect he thereby privileged the perspective of his other, less publicly celebrated friend, Henry James, by nailing Mark Twain to the wall. That, indeed, was James's "Mark Twain," as *The American* clearly enough reveals, and it may have been Howells's also, despite his friendly (and posthumous) memoir, art being finally a golden ghetto in which tastelessness may be tastefully displayed.

NOTES

1. Edwin H. Cady, *The Road to Realism* (Syracuse: Syracuse University Press, 1956), pp. 243–5, Kenneth Lynn, *William Dean Howells: An American Life* (New York: Harcourt Brace Jovanovich, 1971), pp. 280–3, and Kermit Vanderbilt, *The Achievement of William Dean Howells* (Princeton, N.J.: Princeton University Press, 1968), pp. 96–105, all allude to this incident and speculate, variously, on its causes and consequences. But only Vanderbilt structures his discussion of *Silas Lapham* entirely on this complex and speculative issue, which he relates to Howells's anxieties over the Jewish and Irish "problems" as well as to his troubled allegiance to the Brahmins of Boston and his growing social consciousness. My own discussion depends heavily on Vanderbilt's detailed documentation and discussion, though our emphasis and conclusions differ considerably. Let me state here my indebtedness also to my colleague, David Leverenz, whose reading and suggestions regarding a draft of this essay resulted in strategic revisions.

2. Cf. also Corey's earlier remark, in reference to Lapham's use of the landscape for his advertisements: "He isn't to my taste, though he might be ever so much to my conscience," a division central to Howells's own conception of Lapham (p. 67). We are earlier told of Silas and his wife that "they had a crude taste in architecture, and they admired the worst," having "decorated their house with the costliest and most abominable frescoes" (pp. 34, 27). There is also a suggestion that the placing of the religious symbols in their parlor was perhaps more for show than spiritual sustenance, being "kneeling figures

which turned their backs upon the company within doors, and represented allegories of Faith and Prayer to people without" (p. 215).

3. In his introduction to his edition of *The Rise of Silas Lapham* (New York: Penguin Books, 1983), Kermit Vanderbilt touches briefly on the resemblance between Lapham and Mark Twain (p. x). For Mrs. Aldrich's anecdote, see Lilian W. Aldrich, *Crowding Memories* (Boston: Houghton Mifflin, 1920), pp. 128–32.

4. The reference to Sellers is on p. 283, to Twain's "The Celebrated Jumping Frog of Calaveras County" on p. 86, to the coincidental dates on pp. 10, 12. Penelope's curious qualities of voice are described on pp. 133, 164, and 221.

5. See Vanderbilt, pp. 135–6, n. 54, who also identifies the episode of the dinner and its aftermath in *Silas Lapham* with "the moment when the bottom dropped out" of Howells's life. See also Henry Nash Smith, "That Hideous Mistake of Poor Clemens's," *Harvard Library Bulletin* 9 (Spring 1955): 145–80, and Lynn, *Howells*, p. 173.

6. Lynn, *Howells*, p. 177.

7. The debate over cross-cultural marriages would continue in American literature. In 1902, Owen Wister, James's friend and Howells's protégé, effected a match between a Virginia-born cowboy and a schoolteacher from Vermont, a symbolic union of regional and cultural differences to which James (in a letter to Wister) politely demurred, remaining consistent to his earlier program. Wister's friend and illustrator, Frederic Remington, also objected, and in his novel, *John Ermine of the Yellowstone* (1902), mounted a rebuttal, following the Jamesian pattern of putting a tragic end to a mistaken, transcultural romance, lending it an added dimension of miscegenation by giving his hero an Indian upbringing, in essence returning to the purely miscegenatory burden of Cooper's *Last of the Mohicans* (1826). (See my introduction to *The Virginian* [New York: Penguin Books, 1988], pp. xviii–xx.) Vanderbilt (p. 127) notes that although an alert reader of the *Century* serialization of *Silas Lapham* had informed Howells that Bartley Hubbard's allusion to "Daisy Millerism" was an anachronism, he did not expunge it from the final version of the novel, although other material was revised: "Howells, with surprising stubbornness, maintained that the allusion to Daisy Miller was indispensable and could not be deleted." In a work in progress, from which this present essay is excerpted, I hope to show that a number of characteristic nineteenth-century novels exhibit structural flaws directly related to their failures to accommodate the formulaics of fiction to the problematics of racial, class, and cultural conflicts, taboos disruptive of aesthetic decorum.

4

The Economy of Pain: Capitalism, Humanitarianism, and the Realistic Novel

WAI-CHEE DIMOCK

A T ONE of the most touching moments in *The Rise of Silas Lapham*, the Laphams, feeling wretched about the drastic new development in their daughters' marital fortunes, go to consult the Reverend Sewell. The minister offers his counsel in the form of a hypothetical question. If somebody else had come to them, with the same unhappy discovery that the presumptive suitor of one daughter was really courting the other, what would they have said? Wouldn't they have come up with some kind of moral arithmetic to solve the problem? As Sewell sees it, that arithmetic is one that would seek to minimize pain:

> "One suffer instead of three, if none is to blame?" suggested Sewell. "That's sense, and that's justice. It's the economy of pain which naturally suggests itself, and which would insist upon itself, if we were not all perverted by traditions which are the figment of the shallowest sentimentality."[1]

As a way of managing the suffering of others, Sewell's "economy of pain" is a truly indispensable vehicle. The sentient and the economic are not usually seen in such close conjunction: Sewell not only mentions them in the same breath but also uses them to justify and reinforce each other. If his concern with pain reflects a humane sensibility, his emphasis on economy, on the distribution and management of pain, bespeaks another influence as well. Neither strictly a model for moral conduct nor strictly a model for economic organization, Sewell's economy of pain works, instead, as a combination of the two. We might think of it as a kind of moral economy, a model whose claim to justice rests on its ability to conjoin the moral and the economic, or rather, on the fact that, under its dispensation, the moral and the economic need no conjoining at all, because they are already one and the same: What is economic here *is* also what is moral.[2] This neat arrangement comes about because, according to Sewell, suffering can become morally acceptable only when it is economically organized. Its rationale rests on its rationality. Such a model obviously tries to minimize pain, but even as it does so, it also confers legitimacy on what it minimizes. Because one is inflicting as little pain as possible, what one does inflict becomes correspondingly acceptable. In Sewell's model, then, resource allocation and moral adjudication turn out to be identical activities, because in perfecting the former one also enforces the latter.

Sewell's economy of pain appears, on this occasion, as a modest proposal concerning only the Laphams. Still, as a way of calibrating, distributing, and legitimizing suffering, its sphere of application would seem much wider. In fact, such a way of thinking about pain has a history of its own outside fiction. Simon Nelson Patten, the turn-of-the-century economist and social Darwinist, would soon speak, in terms strikingly similar to Sewell's, of a "pain economy," to be replaced by a "pleasure economy" as society progressed.[3] Less sanguine about such progress, Patten's more famous associate, William Graham Sumner, perhaps the best known social Darwinist in America, concentrated instead on economics of the less pleasurable sort. "Who pays for it?" he asks, repeatedly and always in a tone of gloating malice, in his well-known essay, "The Forgotten Man" (1883). "Paying" is what someone always ends up doing, Sumner argues, because society works by "the balance of the account," and "the advantage of some is won by an equivalent loss of others." It follows then, that "whatever capital you diverted to the support of a shiftless and good-for-nothing person is so much diverted from some other employment," and "if you give a loaf to a pauper," you are in effect "trampling on the Forgotten Man."[4]

Sumner does not speak of an economy of pain, but that is clearly his subject. What incenses him, indeed, is what he perceives to be a gross defect in the existing economy, namely, in its distribution of resources, or, to be more precise, in the negative branch of that activity: in its distribution of pain. Instead of allocating pain to the proper recipients, this economy inflicts it instead on the Forgotten

Man, that "clean, quiet, virtuous, domestic citizen" who is the "victim" of the "idle, the intemperate, the extravagant," who is "weighted down . . . with the support of all the loafers," who is made to pay "the penalty while our minds were full of the drunkards, spendthrifts, gamblers."[5] Sumner's accents here are recognizably social Darwinian, but his concerns are by no means exclusively social Darwinian ones. The preoccupation with suffering – with its distribution and legitimacy – was very much a nineteenth-century preoccupation, shared by people of all ideological shades and stripes.[6] This widespread interest in suffering has led one historian, Michael Ignatieff, to call his book on nineteenth-century prison reform *A Just Measure of Pain*.[7] The same phenomenon, showing up in the context of professional medicine, has led another historian, Martin Pernick, to describe as "a calculus of suffering" the practice of medical doctors, who, in their shifting standard on the uses of anesthetics, would seem to be engaged in the same task of measuring and meting out pain. Apparently it was common practice in the United States, from the 1840s through the 1880s, for doctors to administer anesthetics to some patients and not to others. Such a practice, which assumed that "different types of people differed in their sensitivity to pain," obviously had "implications reach[ing] far beyond anesthesia," as Pernick rightly observes.[8] In their operating theater, it would seem, doctors were puzzling over the same logistics of suffering that elsewhere preoccupied prison reformers, social Darwinists, and the Reverend Sewell.[9]

Such a widespread interest in pain was not altogether surprising. The nineteenth century, an age of rapid industrial expansion, was also an age of industrial poverty and urban slums, haunted both by the growing proximity and visibility of human suffering, and by the perception that this suffering was not just an isolated phenomenon, but part of a symptomatic network.[10] Such a perception, which emphasized the connections among things, was especially important to the nineteenth century, so much so that we might think of it as a nineteenth-century cognitive style. This is especially true of late nineteenth-century America, which, as historians tell us, was rapidly transformed from a nation of "island communities" to a nation of corporate interdependence, organized into a vast interlocking network by the advent of the railroad, the emergence of government bureaucracy, and the growth of big business.[11] As local livelihood became tied to distant events – to the Wall Street crash of 1873, for instance, or the bitter railroad strikes of 1877 – local welfare also seemed bound up with the welfare of strangers, strangers unknown, unloved, unconscionably numerous. Nineteenth-century Americans, in short, had to adapt not only to an expanded geographical universe but, even more crucially, to an expanded causal universe, in which human agency, social relations, and moral responsibility all had to be redefined. An ever-widening field of causality could be both inspiring and scary, and those confronted with it reacted variously, often antithetically. Nativist sentiments, noticeably strong during this period, registered one kind of response: Immigrants, after all, embodied all that was alien and threatening in a world grown too large and complex.[12] Humanitarian sentiments, equally strong during the same period, registered another kind of response: accepting causal connections even among the seemingly unconnected, reformers proceeded to act upon them, treating the welfare of the poor and weak as their own responsibility.

Howells himself would write about this sense of human connectedness in his next book, *The Minister's Charge* (1886). Published just a year after *The Rise of Silas Lapham*, this novel shares some of the themes and characters of its predecessor, and, as it happens, it is once again the Reverend Sewell who is made to deliver the book's central statement. "Everybody's mixed up with everybody else," he observes with admirable succinctness, in a sermon titled "Complicity."[13] Complicity, the condition of being all mixed up, is indeed an inescapable fact in Howells, and the agonizing problems of both *The Minister's Charge* and *The Rise of Silas Lapham* can all be traced to it. Those problems, in turn, inspire Sewell to come up with a vehicle of arbitration: an economy of pain. Even within the space of these two novels, then, a double pattern begins to emerge: a problem and a solution, something that produces moral entanglements and something that releases those entanglements. Within the terms of our discussion, we might say that, on the one hand, there is a movement toward expanded connectedness, which implicates everyone, and makes everyone responsible for everyone else. Complementing it, however, is a movement in the opposite direction, a movement that restores limits, that tries to minimize not only suffering but also the obligations that suffering entails.

Taken together, these double motions in Howells would seem to constitute a self-limiting cognitive structure, which not only honors moral responsibilities but also makes sure that they will be kept within bounds. Such a structure casts an interesting light on the recent debate among historians about the cognitive conditions for moral responsibility, a debate that has ignited the pages of the *American Historical Review*. What sparked it was an important theoretical essay, "Capitalism and the Origins of the Humanitarian Sensibility," by Thomas Haskell. Haskell argues that a particular form of moral sensibility, in this case, a capacity for humanitarian action, can flourish only within the cognitive universe of a particular form of economic life, in this case, capitalism. Capitalism rewards those who can think in terms of distant events, who can connect things across space and time, and, in doing so, it helps to enlarge not only "the range of causal perceptions" but also the range of assumed obligations. What capitalism accomplishes is not just an economic revolution but, even more crucially, a cognitive revolution. Out of this revolution, Haskell argues, a "new moral universe" is born, where "failing to go to the aid of a suffering stranger might become an unconscionable act." Contrary, then, to the common assumption that capitalism encourages greed and selfishness, Haskell argues that the opposite is true. Indeed, according to him, "the emergence of a market-oriented form of life gave rise to new habits of causal attribution that set the stage for humanitarianism."[14]

Haskell's argument is obviously designed to outrage his colleagues, but there is something compelling about it all the same. Indeed, we only have to think of the Ford, Rockefeller, and Carnegie foundations to see that there is indeed a vital link between capitalism and humanitarianism. Haskell's paradigm is valuable in suggesting one sort of historical linkage, a cognitive linkage, between a form of economic life and a form of moral sensibility, but other linkages, and other collateral provisions, must be recognized as well in this complex and living genealogy. Without disagreeing with Haskell, then, I would like to complicate his model by sug-

71

gesting one such collateral provision, one that posits capitalism not only as an *enabling* influence on humanitarianism but also as a *limiting* condition, not only its cognitive ground, but also its cognitive boundary. There is a limit beyond which humanitarianism will not go. And, to see how that limit works, and how it is instituted as a cognitive provision, it is useful, I think, to look at the economy of pain, because such an economy, in its ability to minimize not only suffering but also obligation, is also a crucial instrument for establishing boundaries and maintaining limits. It is a crucial instrument, we might say, for preventing moral responsibilities from becoming moral liabilities.

Such a safety mechanism is central, I suggest, to the workings of capitalism. Indeed the corporation itself, as a legal entity, is invented to provide just that mechanism in the legal domain.[15] In the moral domain, an analogous mechanism must exist as well. Here too, a means for limiting liabilities – something like the moral equivalent of the corporation – must be invented, because, in order to work as a moral economy (rather than a moral anarchy), capitalism must pragmatically restrict the range of obligations that it constitutionally enlarges. One of the most popular works by nineteenth-century moral philosophers, not surprisingly, was Francis Wayland's *The Limitation of Human Responsibility* (1838). Wayland argued, as did many of his colleagues, that, whereas "our responsibility for the temper of mind is unlimited and universal, our responsibility for the outward act is limited and special."[16] In other words, as far as our intentions are concerned, unlimited responsibility applies; as far as our actions are concerned, however, that responsibility can be no more than a case of limited liability. And, to keep the liability firmly within limits, some rationale for suffering – some way of making it accountable and even acceptable – must complement the humanitarian sensibility as its check and correlative.

It is fitting, then, that the Reverend Sewell should give voice both to a doctrine of complicity and to an economy of pain. It is fitting, too, that the nineteenth century should be both an age of humanitarian reform and an age given over to the idea that there might be a differential scale to pain: that different people might feel it differently, and that the more civilized races, in particular, might have a greater susceptibility. Writing in 1806, Thomas Trotter, surgeon to the British fleet, worried that the march of civilization would produce a "general effeminacy," since it "never fail[s] to induce a delicacy of feeling, that disposes alike to more acute pain, as to more exquisite pleasure."[17] Others shared his concern. Throughout the century, physicians lamented that "civilized life" had heightened the sensitivity to pain, and that childbirth had become "exceedingly painful . . . especially in the upper walks of life."[18] As late as 1892, S. Weir Mitchell, the founder of American neurology (and the implied villain in Charlotte Perkins Gilman's *The Yellow Wallpaper*), would make the same argument, in an essay with a self-explanatory title, "Civilization and Pain." "In our process of being civilized we have won intensified capacity to suffer," he wrote. "The savage does not feel pain as we do."[19]

The "savage [who] does not feel pain" included Indians, who could "inure themselves to burning part of their bodies with fire," and blacks, who having a "greater insensibility to pain," could "submit to and bear the infliction of the rod with a surprising degree of resignation, and even cheerfulness."[20] But cheerfulness in the face of bodily affliction was by no means limited to these two obvious groups of savages. "Savagery" was a remarkably elastic category in the nineteenth century. It was understood to exist, for instance, also in urban slums, whose population, according to Horace Mann, was rapidly "falling back into the conditions of half-barbarous or of savage life."[21] And, not surprisingly, the category of the "insentient" turned out to be as elastic and commodious. It did not take much stretching to apply it elsewhere, as in this characteristic statement by John W. De Forest, a wealthy Connecticut citizen and writer of realistic novels. "We waste unnecessary sympathy on poor people," he said. "A man is not necessarily wretched because he is cold and hungry and unsheltered; provided these circumstances usually attend him, he gets along very well with them."[22]

By a magical calculus, then, insensitivity to pain would seem proportional to the incidence of pain. Those who had the most to suffer turned out also to be least hurt by it. For De Forest, this meant that the sufferings of others were not really sufferings, after all, and that he was under no obligation to relieve those sufferings.

De Forest's antihumanitarianism is well served by his economy of pain, but it would be wrong to assume that such an economy was invoked only by the like-minded, those reluctant to "waste unnecessary sympathy." Lydia Maria Child, an abolitionist with no lack of humanitarian sympathy, nevertheless saw a correlation between the hardships of black slaves and their supposed insensitivity to pain. For her, it was a "merciful arrangement of Divine Providence, by which the acuteness of sensibility is lessened when it becomes merely a source of suffering."[23] Like De Forest, then, Child believed that those who had the most to suffer were least able to feel it, except that in her version, of course, the slaves' insensitivity proved that slavery was abominable, and that abolition was imperative.

In short, to support their respective arguments, both De Forest and Child find it convenient to assume an economy of pain, which, oddly enough, seems to underwrite both positions. If it promotes Child's humanitarianism on the one hand, it also justifies De Forest's antihumanitarianism on the other. The former's expanded commitments and the latter's curtailed obligations both have a function within this all accommodating calculus. It would be a mistake, indeed, to associate such an economy of pain either exclusively with De Forest, or exclusively with Child, because neither is an exception, and both are necessary to what is essentially a self-divided and self-limiting structure of obligation. De Forest, from this perspective, represents not so much a negation of Child as a supplement to her, not so much a counter as a codicil.

The same self-limiting structure, the same double provision for expanded commitments and curtailed obligations, governs the realistic novel as well. The novel's moral imagination, its devotion to human connectedness and human responsibility, is well known, of course. In its richly involved (and sometimes richly improbable) plots, in its far-flung attribution of cause and consequence, it certainly attests to the "expanded range of causal perception" Haskell describes. And yet, as we intuitively sense and as Leo Bersani has brilliantly demonstrated, the novel's fictive universe is not only conspicuously accommodating, it is also incessantly controlled.[24] In fact, the very form of the novel might be seen as an overdetermined form, a teleological inscription of the ending in the beginning. Given these dual aspects of the novel – its plenitude as well as its regimentation – we might think of it as an uneasy compromise between two contending forces: between the claims of expanded connectedness on the one hand, and the claims of reinstated boundaries on the other, or, within the terms of our discussion, between the claims of moral responsibility and the claims of limited liability.

In the very form of the novel, in its web of causality and its need for closure, we see a universe of alternating expansion and contraction that would seem to correspond, more or less, to the alternately expanding and contracting cognitive universe that facilitates both capitalism and humanitarianism. Against our current emphasis on "ideology" or "epistemology," then, I would offer the "cognitive" as a more fundamental as well as more encompassing category to think about the literary form.[25] The genesis of form, both social forms and literary forms, is no more than the materialization of the cognitive. From this perspective, the formal coordinates of the novel – the temporal and spatial boundaries within which an event is linked to an antecedent or an adjacent event, seen as sequential to or congruent with something else – would seem parallel to the cognitive coordinates by which a society organizes itself, by which it defines its radius of pertinence and limits of probability.

More than any other American author, William Dean Howells championed the realistic novel, and he did so on formal grounds. The virtue of the novel, according to him, lies in its formal amplitude, its ability to encompass all things and connect all mankind. The aim of the realistic novel is to "widen the bounds of sympathy," he says, to proclaim the "equality of things and the unity of men." Everything is pertinent to the realist: "In life he finds nothing insignificant. . . . He cannot look upon human life and declare this thing or that thing unworthy of notice."[26] But the realistic novel is not just commodious in its outlook; it is also equipped to connect what it sees, to affirm "those finer and higher aspects which unite rather than sever humanity."[27] Howells himself was so enchanted by the idea of human connectedness that he even proposed, in a hyperbolical moment, that, as a writer, he was "merely a working-man," "allied to the great mass of wage-workers," and was, moreover, "glad and proud to be of those who eat their bread in the sweat of their own brows." He urged other writers to think of themselves in the same way, "to feel the tie that binds us to all the toilers of the shop and field, not as a galling chain, but as a mystic bond."[28]

Howells's remarks are important not only because they clarify his own principles of composition, but also because the qualities he admires have been accepted, for the most part, as the governing attributes of the realistic novel.[29] Those attributes are indeed striking, and not to be disputed. But it is also important, I think, to treat them not just as qualities peculiar to the novel and limited to the novel, but as indexes to a larger mental universe, in which such novelistic attributes satisfy and explain, appear meaningful and right.

The Rise of Silas Lapham is a representative text in this regard, because its formal amplitude is so evident. The book is what we might call a "loose, baggy monster" (to borrow Henry James's general description of the novel). And, as baggy monsters go, it is even worse than others – primarily because of two subplots, one only marginally related to the main story, and the other apparently not related at all.[30] The first has to do with Milton K. Rogers, a former partner of Silas Lapham's, squeezed out by him when the business began to prosper, who returns to feed on Lapham's guilt and to borrow money from him. This borrowing helps to bring about Lapham's downfall, and Rogers, in that regard, has something to contribute to the plot. His contribution is not strictly necessary, however, because bad investments alone could have ruined Lapham, and the plot hardly depends on the exertions of this unlucky, unlovely creature. Even so, Rogers is more integral to the story than Miss Dewey, a typist in Lapham's office and the center of the other subplot. *Her* only contribution to the story is to provoke Mrs. Lapham into a fit of unfounded jealousy, but otherwise she seems completely superfluous.

In their semidetached state, Rogers and Miss Dewey would seem to confirm our usual view of the realistic novel as a commodious vessel, whose formal identity lies in the abundance, perhaps even superfluity, of its details. And yet, if we think of the subplot not as a thematic appendage to the main plot but as its structural complement, the seemingly gratuitous complications turn out to be not gratuitous but necessary, if only as the negative condition of possibility for the main plot. For the subplot, in its unwieldy, unwarranted complications, would seem to represent the very circumstances – an expanded, and ultimately untenable, radius of pertinence – which the main plot must rectify, contain, counteract. Within the terms of this essay, we might also say that the subplot, as a field of ever-widening entanglements, is also the formal register of the novel's humanitarian impulse: a network of causal connections as well as moral obligations that must ultimately be kept in check.[31] That double movement – an initial expansiveness as well as an eventual retrenchment – is exactly how the two subplots work in *The Rise of Silas Lapham.*

The tenuous ties that connect Rogers and Miss Dewey to the story are important, then, precisely because they *are* tenuous, because they define a radius of pertinence so wide as to appear limitless. In such a world of causal infinitude, human responsibility becomes infinitely problematic. Is Lapham still responsible for the fate of Rogers after all these years? How long should he keep on making amends, and how far must he go? That is the very question Mrs. Lapham asks, and her answer is unequivocal. "I want you should ask yourself," she urges her husband, "whether Rogers would ever have gone wrong, or got into these ways of his, if it hadn't been for your forcing him out of the business when you did. I want you should think whether you're not responsible for everything he's done since" (p. 262).

Mrs. Lapham has "a woman's passion for fixing responsibility" (p. 277), Howells tells us, and she certainly seems to be indulging it on this occasion. Still, her passion turns out to be more sporadic than we might think. She has no desire to "fix responsibility," for instance, when the responsibility involves taking care of the widow and child of a dead army buddy. In fact, she is as vehemently opposed, on this point, as she is vehemently insistent on the other. "One of the things she had to fight [Lapham] about was that idea of his that he was bound to take care of Jim Millon's worthless wife and her child because Millon had got the bullet that was meant for him" (p. 340). As far as she is concerned, this is just "willful, wrong-headed kind-heartedness" (p. 341) on Lapham's part, because he has no moral responsibility to speak of in this case, and no reason to "look after a couple of worthless women who had no earthly claim on him" (p. 362). Fight as she does, however, she cannot "beat [the idea] out of" her husband, because, on this occasion at least, Lapham is operating in a wider causal universe than her own. Seeing himself as the cause of Jim Millon's death, he puts himself under a moral obligation toward the dead man's family. That is why Miss Dewey is in his office to begin with; she is Jim Millon's daughter, and Lapham feels "bound to take care of" her and her mother. The subplot revolving around the typist, then, turns out to be exactly analogous to the one revolving around Rogers. In both bases, a distant event is evoked to reveal a network of complications and entanglements, giving rise to a universe of ever-receding and ever-expanding causality, a universe of unlimited connections, and unlimited liability.

It is the unlimited liability, of course, that precipitates Lapham's downfall. The causal universe he inhabits is not only fearfully expansive but also fatally expensive. Moral responsibilities here have a way of becoming financial liabilities, because both Rogers and Miss Dewey (as well as her mother) use their moral claims to ask for money, a fact significant in itself and suggestive of the problematic Howells means to set up. Lapham speaks both too prophetically and too soon, then, when he says, "I'm glad to have that old trouble healed up. I don't think I ever did Rogers any wrong. . . . but if I *did* do it – if I did – I'm willing to call it square, if I never see a cent of my money back again" (p. 132). The money that he will "never see a cent of back again" turns out to be the sum total of his fortune, for Milton K. Rogers, Lapham later realizes, has a way of "let[ting] me in for this thing, and that thing, and [has] bled me every time" (p. 274). Lapham's moral economy is, without question, an economy of expenditure, and even though Howells approves of it, at least in this instance, it is ultimately untenable as anything other than a cautionary tale, something others must try to avoid.[32] Lapham himself suggests as much. All his troubles began with "Rogers in the first place," he says. "It was just like starting a row of bricks. I tried to catch up, and stop 'em from going, but they all tumbled, one after another. It wasn't in the nature of things that they could be stopped till the last brick went" (p. 364).

A domino theory of moral responsibility is clearly a frightening prospect. But if so, the very terms of Howells's problematic would seem already to suggest a remedy. If moral responsibilities tend to get out of hand by mutating into financial liabilities, then the solution must work in the opposite direction, which is to say, it must try to rectify the moral by way of the economic. In short, by dramatizing the permeable relation between the moral and the economic, and by focusing on liability as a problem in moral conduct, Howells not only makes morality a vital issue in business dealings, he also makes economics a vital instrument in moral arbitration.[33] The Reverend Sewell is speaking not just for himself, then, but equally for Howells, when he urges upon the Laphams an economy of pain. Such an economy, in its ability to manage both suffering and obligation, would have saved Lapham not only from his financial woes but also from his moral agonies.

Of course, it is not Lapham's good fortune to benefit from such an economy, nor is he the intended beneficiary. Sewell has in mind a different problem and a different set of clients. Not the Laphams themselves, but their offspring, Penelope, and not the elder Coreys either, but their offspring, Tom, will stand to benefit, both from Sewell's proposed economy of pain and from the actual novelistic economy that is *The Rise of Silas Lapham*. Such a differential pattern in the assignment of benefits is itself interesting, but even more interesting is its double effect, at once minimizing and legitimizing pain. This effect should alert us to the degree to which every novelist is an economist: not only in the commerce of books but, even more basically, in the composition of books. For in the composing of a plot, in orchestrating the destinies of his characters, distributing benefits and assigning suffering, the novelist is necessarily a practicing economist, enforcing some model of resource management. Indeed, if the task of the novelist is, as Howells says, to portray "human feelings in their true proportion and relation" (p. 197), some principle of apportionment, some way of adjudicating rival claims and affixing balances, is crucial. "Resource allocation" might turn out to be as much a necessity in the composition of a novel as it is in the composition of a society. If so, the problems of political economy, the problems of distribution and legitimacy, would seem as intrinsic to the former as to the latter.

To the extent that the novel is itself an economy, our usual emphasis on its *thematic* referentiality would seem quite inadequate. What we need as well, I think, is a theory about its *formal* referentiality: a theory about the novel form as a system of distribution and adequation, and about its relation, as such, to the more general system of distribution and adequation that obtains outside the province of fiction.[34] We might even argue for a direct link between the formal arrangements inside a novel, arrangements that guarantee its poetic justice, and the social arrangements outside a novel, arrangements designed for the same end. From the standpoint of practical criticism, what this suggests is that we might want to focus less on the actions and psychologies of individual characters and more on their aggregate configuration, their mutualities and equivalences within a pattern of correlated gain and loss.

Some such pattern, in fact, is what Tom Corey notices, and what gives him hope, as he contemplates the synchronized gain and loss that seem to have overtaken himself and his employer, Silas Lapham. "Lapham's potential ruin" might turn out to be his own salvation, Tom thinks, because this is a case where "another's disaster would befriend him, and give him the opportunity to prove the unselfishness of his constancy" (p. 272). This is not just wishful thinking either, because it in fact happens: Lapham's downfall does indeed "befriend" Corey, and his marriage to Penelope does indeed take place, to the tune of his father-in-law's financial disaster. In some mysterious fashion, then, the two events seem to have balanced each other, in a remote and yet correlated proportionality. And yet, simply to note that fact does not quite settle the question, because, from our perspective, what is most interesting is not so much the proportionality itself as the ground on which it is computed, the ground on which one event is judged the equivalent of the other. In what sense, and by what calculus, does Lapham's financial disaster (not to mention the elder Corey's afflicted sensibility) answer to the marital bliss of Tom and Penelope? What rate of exchange, to put the question most bluntly, measures those two events and certifies their proportionality?

To ask such questions is obviously to think of the novel form as a system of symbolic equivalents, in which disparate events tally with each other, compensate for each other, and balance each other, both as a matter of figuration and as a matter of configuration. Such an approach is not without its hazards, of course; there is always the danger, for instance, of being reductive, of analyzing the literary form only in terms of its lowest common denominator. But there are also advantages to this method, one of which is that it enables us to reconstruct, through the novel form, something like its cognitive precondition, the assumptions about identity and difference, about congruence and commensurability, that make the very creation of form possible. In short, in thinking about the novel as a system of symbolic equivalents, we might also be able to think, more generally, about the grounds for equivalence that govern both the narrative arrangements inside fiction and the social arrangements outside it.

In *The Rise of Silas Lapham,* the grounds for equivalence are especially interesting, because they require, more specifically, the yoking together of pleasure and pain, in a narrative balance. Such an arrangement (whose goal, after all, is to make the pleasure of some characters equivalent to the pain of others) might seem bizarre in one sense, but it is by no means unthinkable, because, as we shall see, neither the pain nor the pleasure here turns out to be unmixed, and, being so compounded and confounded, they are also infinitely fluid, and infinitely amenable to the postulate of equivalence. Positing equivalences, then, I would argue, is the central task of *The Rise of Silas Lapham,* just as it is, more generally, the task of the realistic novel. This impulse, to create identity out of difference, explains, I think, why the nineteenth-century novel gives us so few straightforward "happy endings," and why the ones that we do get are often so tepid and so unsatisfactory that their pleasure seems virtually a kind of pain. The well-known marriages that conclude nineteenth-century novels – between Fanny Price and Edmund Bertram, between Jane Eyre and Mr. Rochester, between Dorothea Brooke and Will Ladislaw – are "happy endings" only in form; in any other respect they hardly deserve the title. Within this context, the famous last line of *The Bostonians* must serve as an extreme epigraph to the genre. When Verena goes off with Basil Ransom, she is discovered, James tells us, to be "in tears." And he goes on, "It is to be feared that with the union, so far from brilliant, into which she was about to enter, these were not the last she was destined to shed."[35]

Howells does not say that about Penelope, of course, and we have every expectation that she will fare better than Verena Tarrant. And yet it is interesting that, even in *The Rise of Silas Lapham*, a book that otherwise has little in common with *The Bostonians*, Howells should find it incumbent upon himself to supply his "happy ending" with some measure of unhappiness.[36] "The marriage came after so much sorrow and trouble," Howells tells us, "and the fact was received with so much misgiving for the past and future, that it brought Lapham none of the triumph" (p. 359). The same is true, needless to say, on the side of the Coreys: polite tolerance is all they can muster toward their new in-law. As for Penelope herself, when she is finally allowed to go off with Tom, she too, strangely enough, is seen "cry[ing] on his shoulder" (p. 361). That activity is perhaps more appropriate to Verena, but it is not entirely out of place in Penelope either, because her case, as we have seen, is one of mixed blessing, of "painful pleasure," something nineteenth-century novelists apparently feel obligated to concoct at the end of their stories.

But if pleasure shows up in the realistic novel as mixed pleasure, the obverse is just as true. By the same logic, pain also will not be unadulterated pain, or at least it will not register as such. Instead, it too will bring along a kind of compensation, so that, far from being an unmitigated disaster, it might seem a blessing in disguise. To be crude about it, we might even say that, in many nineteenth-century novels, there is a trade-off between suffering and edification. Pain is the "price" one has to pay in exchange for a certain moral elevation. This phenomenon is probably familiar enough to need no illustration. Within this context, *The Rise of Silas Lapham* must seem an exemplary story, because the "rise" that is advertised in the title, the moral ascent of its main character, is of course predicated on (and purchased by) the pain that character is made to endure. What makes Lapham's fictive trajectory possible, then, is a crucial and animating process of exchange: an exchange between beginnings and endings, between what he starts out with and what he ends up with.

From this perspective, Lapham's beginnings — the assets that accompany him when he first appears — are especially worthy of notice. And *assets* is the right word because, in the first part of the book, Lapham is noticeably well endowed: endowed, that is, with bodily parts that are not only conspicuous but downright obtrusive. Over and over again, we hear about his "bulk" (p. 4), his "huge foot" (p. 3), his "No. 10 boots" (p. 6). He is in the habit of "pound[ing] with his great hairy fist" (p. 3), and, instead of closing the door with his hands, he uses "his huge foot" (p. 3). When he talks to Bartley Hubbard, he puts "his huge foot close to Bartley's thigh" (p. 14). Lapham's body is prominently on display in the opening chapter, and the rest of the book bears out this initial portrait. We continue to hear about his "hairy paws" (p. 84), his "ponderous fore-arms" (p. 202), and his "large fists hang[ing] down . . . like canvased hams" (p. 188). It is inconceivable that Bromfield Corey would have appeared in this light, not only because Boston Brahmins do not have "hairy paws," but because Boston Brahmins are not described in bodily terms at all. Lapham's attributes, then, turn out to be less a matter of neutral portrayal than of strategic representation. He comes with a body, a body grossly physical and grossly visible, and that is the most significant fact about him. His physicality stands as the sum and measure of who he is.

In this context, it is especially ominous that Lapham's body is so often linked with his failures to "rise" — failures first literal and then not so literal. When Bartley Hubbard shows up at the office, for instance, Lapham "did not rise from the desk at which he was writing, but he gave Bartley his left hand for welcome, and he rolled his large head in the direction of a vacant chair" (p. 3). Similarly, when he needs to close the door, he does not rise, but "put[s] out his huge foot" to push it shut (p. 4). So far, Lapham's failure to rise is literally just that: He does not get up from his chair, his body stays put. Things become more worrisome, however, when this bodily inertia becomes metaphorical. Lapham's head, we are told, rests on "a short neck, which does not trouble itself to rise far" (p. 4). Some tyranny of physique seems to be keeping him down, and so we are not surprised to learn that he had failed to rise on another occasion as well, when it would have behooved his moral character to do so. Years ago, when he had to decide whether to keep Rogers on or to force him out, Lapham found that he could not "choose the ideal, the unselfish part in such an exigency" – in short, that he "could not rise to it" (p. 50). It is a fatal mistake, of course, although, given his beginnings, given the negative assets that dominate him from the first, it is no more than what we might expect. With a body like his, failure to rise is all but a foregone conclusion.

And yet Lapham does eventually rise, and indeed is destined to do so, as the title promises. Between the unrisen Lapham at the beginning of the book and the risen Lapham at the end, some momentous change has taken place. We might think of it, in fact, not just as a change but as an exchange – an exchange of person-. ality traits – because he is able to rise only insofar as he is able to trade one set of attributes for another. What he possesses at the end is no longer the gross animal vitality he once flaunted, but rather, "a sort of pensive dignity that . . . sometimes comes to such natures after long sickness, when the animal strength has been taxed and lowered" (p. 349). In short, a gain and a loss seem to have occurred somewhere, "taxing" and "lowering" Lapham's animal strength to augment his moral capital.

Exchange of this sort is what constitutes a moral economy in Howells, I would suggest, and the mechanics for it turns out to be straightforward enough. As Howells's allusion to "long sickness" suggests, what facilitates the exchange, the conversion from the animal to the moral, is a severe affliction, a just measure of pain, we might even say. Of course, as we also know, the long sickness in question is not physical sickness, but mental agony, the sort of sickness that befalls us when all our money disappears, a conceit borne out by Lapham's complaint that Rogers has "bled" him. Blood-letting, it would seem, is the means to moral elevation, because according to the internal economy that regulates Lapham's being, animal strength and moral capital turn out to be symbolic equivalents, and the gain in one cannot be effected without a corresponding loss in the other. Suffering ennobles, then, precisely because, by virtue of the loss that it entails, it is also able to bring forth a new ratio in one's composition of character, a new balance of attributes, and a gain commensurate with the loss. Understood as such, suffering never exists in isolation, but always in partnership with something else. It is only half the equation in an economy of pain, the other half being not only its complement but also its compensation.

We have arrived then, once again, at a paradoxical situation where things are strangely mixed up, where pain seems indistinguishable from pleasure. This is the mirror image, of course, of the economy of pleasure. Just as the latter mixes pleasure with pain and turns every happy ending into a tearful event, so the former mixes pain with pleasure and turns every disaster into a hidden blessing. It is just this sort of logic that makes Lapham's story a comedy, in spite of its palpable hardships. From one point of view, of course, Lapham has suffered much: He has gone bankrupt, and his paint business has fallen apart. From another point of view, however, such suffering might look like a kind of miraculous salvation. It is the miraculous salvation, in fact, that Lapham notices, when he talks the matter over with the Reverend Sewell at the end of the book: "Seems sometimes as if it was a hole opened for me, and I crept out of it" (p. 365).

Lapham's misfortune turns out not only to have "befriended" Tom Corey, it seems also to have befriended the sufferer himself. Just like pleasure, which is always appropriately diluted, pain too seems to carry its organic anodyne. In this curious mixing of attributes, we see perhaps the most powerful mechanism that secures for the novel its "poetic justice," that makes its unequal distribution of benefits morally acceptable. Since pleasure here has more than its share of pain, and pain more than its share of pleasure, the two are all but similar; they can be tabulated as such, and, more to the point, they can be distributed as such. Penelope going off to Mexico in her painful pleasure and Lapham going back to Vermont in his pleasurable pain are doing the same thing, after all. Their disparate fortunes bespeak no inequity in resource management, because those fortunes, properly tallied, turn out to be pretty much alike.

If we might speak of the "cultural work" of the realistic novel, a crucial part of that work is surely to educate our moral sensibility, to instill in us a capacity for outrage as well as a capacity for acquiescence. In teaching us, as *The Rise of Silas Lapham* does, to think about pleasure and pain not as stark opposites, but as ambiguous compounds, it no doubt helps us to cope with our own suffering. But it helps us too, it would seem, to cope with the suffering of others – to cope with it, in the sense of acceding to it, accounting for it, and learning to see it, as Howells says, in its "true proportion." Suffering measured by such a calculus can no longer be a reproach, and the realistic novel, operating as an economy of pain, turns out to honor the dictates of both capitalism and humanitarianism. Even as it faithfully represents human sufferings, it just as faithfully prevents those sufferings from becoming liabilities.

NOTES

1. *The Rise of Silas Lapham*, ed. Walter J. Meserve and David J. Nordloh (Bloomington: Indiana University Press, 1971); the Viking Penguin offset reproduction (New York: Viking Penguin, 1983), p. 241. All further references to this edition will appear in the text.

2. "Moral Economy" is of course E. P. Thompson's phrase, which he uses in order to emphasize a cultural (as opposed to a purely economic) basis for the pressure exerted by eighteenth-century crowds on market prices. See "The Moral Economy of the English Crowd in the Eighteenth Century," *Past and Present* 50 (1971): 76–136. My own use of the phrase – focusing on the conjunction of the moral and the economic – is different from Thompson's. It reflects, however, the usage of nineteenth-century moral philosophers, many of whom believed, along with Francis Wayland, that "The Principles of Political Economy are so closely analogous to those of Moral Philosophy, that almost every question in one, may be argued on ground belonging to the other." See Francis Wayland, *The Elements of Political Economy* (Boston: Gould, Kendall & Lincoln, 1837), p. vi.

3. Simon Nelson Patten, *The Theory of Social Forces* (Philadelphia: American Academy of Political and Social Science, 1896), esp. pp. 22–4, 52–3, 76–90. I should point out that Patten's emphasis is on abundance rather than scarcity, and hence on the "pleasure economy"

rather than the "pain economy." It is interesting, all the same, to see how his idiom and categories echo the Reverend Sewell's.

4. William Graham Sumner, "The Forgotten Man," in *Social Darwinism: Selected Essays of William Graham Sumner,* ed. Stow Persons (Englewood Cliffs, N.J.: Prentice-Hall, 1963), pp. 121–6.

5. Ibid., p. 123.

6. For a discussion of the centrality of pain to the late nineteenth-century "martial ideal" and "cult of experience," see T. J. Jackson Lears, *No Place of Grace: Antimodernism and the Transformation of American Culture, 1880–1920* (New York: Pantheon, 1981), pp. 117–24.

7. Michael Ignatieff, *A Just Measure of Pain: The Penitentiary in the Industrial Revolution, 1750–1850* (New York: Columbia University Press, 1978).

8. Martin Pernick, *A Calculus of Suffering: Pain, Professionalism, and Anesthesia in Nineteenth-Century America* (New York: Columbia University Press, 1985).

9. My emphasis on the social organization of pain is obviously indebted to Elaine Scarry, *The Body in Pain: The Making and Unmaking of the World* (New York: Oxford University Press, 1985). In historicizing the disposition of pain, however, I hope to modify Scarry's universalizing tendency.

10. See, for instance, Paul Boyer, *Urban Masses and Moral Order in America, 1820–1920* (Cambridge, Mass.: Harvard University Press, 1978).

11. The phrase "island communities" is Robert Wiebe's, from his well-known study, *The Search for Order, 1877–1920* (New York: Hill and Wang, 1967), p. xiii.

12. See, for instance, John Higham, *Strangers in the Land: Patterns of American Nativism, 1860–1925* (New York: Atheneum, 1963).

13. William Dean Howells, *The Minister's Charge,* ed. Howard Munford, David Nordloh, and David Kleinman (Bloomington: Indiana University Press, 1978), p. 139. For an interesting discussion of this novel (focusing on the relation between language and complicity), see Elsa Nettels, *Language, Race, and Social Class in Howells' America* (Louisville: University of Kentucky Press, 1988), pp. 153–162.

14. Thomas Haskell, "Capitalism and the Origins of the Humanitarian Sensibility, Parts 1 & 2," *American Historical Review* 90 (1985): 339–61, 547–66.

15. Of course, "liability" as a legal issue well preceded the emergence of the corporation. In the 1840s, for instance, the advent of the railroad necessitated the establishment of rules of damage to determine the liabilities of railroads, in cases of injury to property, passengers, and

freight. See Leonard W. Levy, *The Law of the Commonwealth and Chief Justice Shaw* (New York: Oxford University Press, 1957), pp. 118–65.

16. Francis Wayland, *The Limitations of Human Responsibility* (Boston: Gould, Kendall & Lincoln, 1838), p. 19.

17. Thomas Trotter, *A View of the Nervous Temperament; Being a Practical Inquiry into the Increasing Prevalence, Prevention, and Treatment of Those Diseases Commonly Called Nervous, Bilious, Stomach & Liver Complaints* (Troy, N.Y.: Wright, Goodenow & Stockwell, 1808), pp. 21–2.

18. See, for instance, Pernick, *A Calculus of Suffering*, pp. 148–57.

19. S. Weir Mitchell, "Civilization and Pain," *Journal of the American Medical Association* 18 (1892): 108.

20. Benjamin Rush, "Medicine among the Indians of North America: A Discussion" (1774), in *Selected Writings*, ed. Dagobert D. Runes (New York: Philosophical Library, 1947), p. 259; A. P. Merrill, "An Essay on Some of the Distinctive Peculiarities of the Negro Race," *Memphis Medical Recorder* 4 (1855); 67, quoted in Pernick, *A Calculus of Suffering*, p. 155.

21. Horace Mann, "Twelfth Annual Report" (1848), in *Annual Reports on Education* (Boston: Lee and Shepard, 1872), p. 676.

22. Letter of De Forest to his brother, November 27, 1863, De Forest Papers, Yale University Library. Quoted in George M. Fredrickson, *The Inner Civil War: Northern Intellectuals and the Crisis of the Union* (New York: Harper & Row, 1965), p. 87.

23. Lydia Maria Child, *An Appeal in Favor of That Class of Americans Called Africans* (Boston: Allen and Ticknor, 1833), pp. 188–9.

24. See, for instance, *A Future for Astyanax: Character and Desire in Literature* (Boston: Columbia University Press, 1976).

25. Here, I have in mind Fredric Jameson, *The Political Unconscious: Narrative as a Socially Symbolic Act* (Ithaca: Cornell University Press, 1981), and Michael McKeon, *The Origins of the English Novel, 1600–1740* (Baltimore: Johns Hopkins University Press, 1987).

26. William Dean Howells, "Editor's Study," *Harper's* 72 (May 1886): 973.

27. William Dean Howells, "Concerning a Counsel of Imperfection," *Literature* 1 (7 April 1899): 290.

28. William Dean Howells, "The Man of Letters as a Man of Business," in *Literature and Life* (New York: Harper, 1902), 33–4.

29. See, for instance, Donald Pizer, *Realism and Naturalism in Nineteenth-Century American Literature* (Carbondale: University of Southern Illinois Press, 1966); Harold Kolb, *The Illusion of Life: American Realism as a Literary Form* (Charlottesville: University Press of Virginia, 1969);

Edwin H. Cady, *The Light of Common Day: Realism in American Fiction* (Bloomington: University of Indiana Press, 1971). For qualifying views, see Kermit Vanderbilt, *The Achievement of William Dean Howells* (Princeton, N.J.: Princeton University Press, 1968); Henry Nash Smith, "Fiction and the American Ideology: The Genesis of Howells' Early Realism," in *The American Self*, ed. Sam Girgus (Albuquerque: University of New Mexico Press, 1981), pp. 43–57; Alan Trachtenberg, *The Incorporation of America* (New York: Hill and Wang, 1982), pp. 182–207.

30. In fact, as Patrick Dooley points out, contemporary readers of Howells "often focused on the love plot [and] all but ignored the bankruptcy plot." See "Nineteenth-Century Business Ethics and *The Rise of Silas Lapham*," *American Studies* 21 (1980): 79–93.

31. In this context, it is interesting to consider Walter Benn Michaels's view of Howells as an author for whom "excess was the enemy." See *"Sister Carrie's* Popular Economy," *Critical Inquiry* 7 (Winter 1980): 373–90. For a related exchange between Walter Benn Michaels and Leo Bersani about excess and containment in nineteenth-century fiction, see *Critical Inquiry* 8 (Autumn 1981): 158–71.

32. Here, I am responding to our current interest in "expenditure" as a central economic category, especially in the works of Marcel Mauss and George Bataille. See, for instance, Mauss, *The Gift: Forms and Functions of Exchange in Archaic Societies*, trans. I. Cunnison (New York: Norton, 1967), and Bataille, "The Notion of Expenditure," in *Visions of Excess: Selected Writings, 1927–1939*, trans. Allan Stoekl (Minneapolis: University of Minnesota Press, 1985), pp. 116–29. My reading of *The Rise of Silas Lapham* suggests, however, that expenditure is not an autonomous phenomenon, but part of a more encompassing (and self-limiting) structure.

33. For another "economic" reading of Howells (focusing on his status as professional writer), see Christopher Wilson, "Markets and Fictions: Howells' Infernal Juggle," *American Literary Realism* 20 (1988): 2–22.

34. My emphasis on the social negotiations of the literary form (if not my specific argument about distribution and adequation) parallels Catherine Gallagher, *The Industrial Reformation of English Fiction: Social Discourse and Narrative Form, 1832–1867* (Chicago: University of Chicago Press, 1985).

35. Henry James, *The Bostonians* (1886) (Middlesex, England: Penguin, 1966), p. 390.

36. Alfred Habegger has also noted the less than happy endings in

Howells and James. He sees those endings, however, as a protest by male authors against the "fantasy" endings of "women's fiction." See his *Gender, Fantasy, and Realism in American Literature* (New York: Columbia University Press, 1982), pp. 109–10.

5

Smiling through Pain: The Practice of Self in *The Rise of Silas Lapham*

DANIEL T. O'HARA

The Puritan wanted to be a man of calling [*Berufsmensch*] – we must be.

— Max Weber

TWO brief scenes from the latter half of *The Rise of Silas Lapham* interest me.[1] In the first scene, Penelope Lapham faces Mr. Corey, the rich young man who loves her but whom everyone else had assumed loved her sister, Irene. He has come to find out why, after his confession of love, Penelope refuses to have anything to do with him, since no one has bothered, especially not his beloved, to explain the confusion to him. "He came toward her, and then stood faltering. A faint smile quivered over her face at the spectacle of his subjection" (p. 253). In the second scene, also involving Penelope (alone with her mother), the girl's faint smile at Corey's subjection returns, only this time in a context that suggests the gradual dissolution of her resolve. When she learns that Corey had offered "on her account" to invest money in her father's business in his time of financial troubles, Penelope twice censures such efforts as vain and silly attempts to change her. However, in "re-peating the censure" the second time, we learn that her mother thinks "her look was not so severe as her tone; she even smiled a little" (p. 302). It seems a change is going to come.

It also appears as if the repetition of the spectacle of another's subjection has the power of changing one's cruel smile into a look that betrays the diminishing severity of such cruelty. What initially is a smiling that arises from the example of one's power to cause another to stage his own subjection transforms itself, when reiter-ated, into a smiling that appears more promising, despite the repetition of the most painful contrary avowals. "Smiling through" in the first sense of "arising from" thus becomes "smiling through" in the second sense of "in spite of appearances to the contrary." A structure of resentment – conditioned by social, cultural, and/or sexual differences in position and power – arises from the assumption of moral superiority that another's willing subjection confirms. This structure, ironically enough, then gives way to a process of sublimation that bit by bit enables one to appreciate the subjected other's generous if misguided sacrifices. And Corey's sacrifices are truly generous, because his father, like his model Mr. Bennett from *Pride and Prejudice,* has spent most of the family fortune in cultivating a life of leisured irony and aesthetic refinement.

In any event, Penelope cannot permit herself to have her rich young man, without a protracted and painful trial of both her own and his motives. "Tears, Idle Tears," an imaginary sentimental novel in a grieving Tennysonian mode, is the immediate source of her inspiration for this course of action. It tells the tale of an old-fashioned heroine and hero who make wildly satisfying but unnecessary sacrifices for each other. In fact, their trial is endless and climaxes in their exorbitant sacrifice of personal happiness for romantic principle. Despite her own better judgment of this novel as incredibly unrealistic, Penelope, the clever, witty sister, nevertheless allows the novel to shape the romantic crisis of *Silas Lapham.*

As Walter Benn Michaels recently notes, however, the novel's "realism" repudiates this romantic subplot. It does so dramatically, by subversively undoing via these scenes of Penelope's resentful cruelty and lessening resolve, the sentimental ideology of heroic self-sacrifice informing popular novels of the time. And it does so discursively, by incorporating critiques of what Reverend Sewell, Howells's apparent spokesman on the topic, refers to as the genre's excessive "'economy of pain'."[2] Sewell complains that popular novels cultivate among the youth a dangerous prevalence of the imagination of self-sacrifice, which can even encourage a sensitive reader like Penelope, in the name of morality, to give up her love, rather than betray her sister's romantic hopes. Penelope thereby makes many others, besides herself, suffer needlessly.

Michaels, following the lead of these critical discussions, reaches the conclusion that the popular novel, with its "monstrously" (Sewell's word) "disproportionate emphasis on love and self-sacrifice, turns out, surprisingly enough, to be the literary equivalent of the greedy and heartless stock market, which produces wealth out of all proportion to labor or merit." Moreover, Michaels continues, "Realism [is] Howells's literary equivalent of the Laphams' domestic economy and of the Reverend Sewell's 'economy of pain.'" Why? Because "[a]ll three stand in precarious opposition to the excesses of capitalism and the sentimental novel or, rather, to the excessiveness that is here seen to lie at the heart of both the economy and the literature."[3] This opposition between realism, precapitalist domestic economy, and a restricted economy of pain; and naturalism, speculative capitalism, and an excessive, nonrestrictive economy of sacrifice is precarious for Michaels because the ideal of intentional self-limitation informing Howells's trinity of traditional values is itself unrealistic, hopelessly outmoded by the emerging culture of mass – and massive – (self-) consumption.

Howells, for Michaels, is thus the exemplar of American realism, a much-disputed term that like naturalism he rightly prefers not to define. Suffice it to say, for Michaels, Howells's fiction, especially *Silas Lapham*, composes a restricted economy of expenditure – psychic, financial, cultural – that harkens back to the precapitalist era of domestic economy, of primitive and prudent enterprise (versus the current gambling speculation), as the utopian moment of active spirit (versus the decadence of the Gilded Age). Realism, as a life-style as well as a literary program, thus stands in critical opposition to the irresponsibly excessive speculation – psychic, financial, cultural – of the emerging imperialist world order. The latter promotes a speculative expenditure standardizing all areas of the culture according to the developing logic of naturalism, which entails both the reification of spirit and the commodity fetishism of animating material things with our alienated desires that Marx analyzes in *Das Kapital*. Turn-of-the-century American literature, for Michaels, bears witness then to and exemplifies this emerging imperialist world order of consumer capitalism.

In this context, the effect of Howells's "realism" can only be to reinforce the processes it condemns, not so much because it produces novels at odds with their own explicit intentions, as because the novels must monumentalize nostalgically a past mode of economic and literary production perversely (because self-defeatingly) valued by these very novels precisely for their supreme irrelevance and original obsolescence. Consequently, what Howells proposes as critical opposition can only result in quixotic evasion. And Michaels's primary point is that such evasive literary transcendence of one's historical moment is simply not a viable possibility because Howells's writing, like all writing, especially since his time, necessarily always already demonstrates the reifying logic of a self-alienating naturalism that fetishizes the desires of and for selfhood. "What kind of work is writing? It is the work of at once producing and consuming the self or, what comes to the same thing, work in the market."[4] And what, then, is the self, according to Michaels? "[A] commodity, a subject in the market."[5] It is this very development, of course, that Michaels sees Howells in *Silas Lapham* vainly opposing with his unrealistic realism of the domestic "economy of pain" that would curb all those "excesses of capitalism and the sentimental novel or, rather, the excessiveness that is here seen to lie at the heart of both the economy and the literature."[6] Thus, Howells's novel makes a perfectly consistent if essentially irrelevant whole, clearly aligning and separating its old-fashioned good values and modern evils, even as it ironically reinforces their actual confusion by its adoption of a purely imaginary, monumentalizing opposition. Like the fiscal conservatism favoring the gold standard of "hard money," "realistic" opposition to the reifying logic of a naturalizing commodity fetishism (the cultural equivalent of wholesale capitalist speculation) can only "assert the ontological impossibility of what was already an historical fact."[7] In this original way, Michaels pragmatically combines neomarxist analyses with deconstructive assumptions about writing and the production of the self to critique Howells's quixotic realism in *Silas Lapham*.

The main problem with this reading is that it ignores the major contradiction in the novel. For, even as the novel dramatically criticizes and releases Penelope from her thralldom to the romantic ideology of moral heroism pervaded by sentimental fiction, *The Rise of Silas Lapham*, in its main plot focusing on the fate of its protagonist's business fortunes, exemplifies as exemplary the excessive "economy of pain" of this very moral heroism by enmeshing the girl's father ever deeper in it. In fact, expectedly, as Lapham's material fortunes fall, he begins to effect the "rise" of the title, morally speaking, just as, unexpectedly, the resentful cruelty of Penelope's romantic principle of heroic sacrifice sublimates itself ironically into a provisional trial of motives that leads to no such heroic catastrophe as her father suffers.

Lapham's "gambling" in the stock market starts to go bad as his former partner's recent speculative ventures also turn sour. This forces Lapham to invest more and more heavily in order to expiate his guilt for originally buying Rogers out as their paint firm was beginning to make big money. The result is that Lapham is now increasingly vulnerable to Rogers, who, to repay what he owes Lapham, sells him at cost a losing venture whose only access road has just been purchased by a railway that can always pressure our hero whenever it wants. The result is that Lapham starts losing more and more capital, and so cannot match the innovations of his new young competitors in the paint business, who can now begin to capture an ever larger share of the market.

Lapham's house of cards now begins to tumble, even as he "accidentally" sets fire to his still incomplete mansion (his "dream-house"), which is totally consumed by the ensuing conflagration and, naturally, no longer covered by insurance. It is at this sentimentally vulnerable point that Rogers melodramatically comes to Lapham representing some English buyers who want to purchase that losing venture Rogers originally sold to Lapham. Lapham refuses to sell at first, then says he will sell only if he can tell whoever the interested buyers are the truth about the ownership of the access road. Lapham insists on doing so because he sees in Rogers's new deal "the very devil" (p. 323) that would rob him of the last shreds of his moral integrity in resentful revenge for past financial wrongs. In essence, Lapham believes Rogers is tempting him to intentionally repeat, on a grander scale, now under dire circumstances, the original wrong he had "unintentionally" committed in better times against his former partner. When Lapham learns that the English buyers don't care about the truth he has to tell about the access road because they represent a group of wealthy English aristocrats who want the land under any circumstances to build a model socialist community, Lapham reverses himself and now refuses to sell anyway. He claims that he would still be responsible for the evil consequences of the utopian aristocrats' foolhardiness, even if he, unlike Rogers, would not be guilty of perpetrating a fraud. Such fineness of conscience, condemning him and his family to bankruptcy and social ruin, now marks Lapham as a person as extravagantly sacrificial in commercial affairs as his daughter aspires, but ironically fails, to become in romantic matters.

Naturally, as Lapham's empire collapses after this great renunciation, the novel celebrates both his final victory over "temptation" and the return of his original enterprising spirit as he moves his paint business, in greatly reduced form, back onto the family farm. The following passage, at this climactic moment, is typical of the psychological realism and moral sentiment endorsed wholeheartedly and elaborately by the novel:

> Perhaps because the process of his ruin had been so gradual, perhaps because the excitement of preceding events had exhausted their capacity for emotion, the actual consummation of his bankruptcy brought a relief, a repose to Lapham and his family, rather than a fresh sensation of calamity. In the shadow of his disaster they returned to something like their old, united life; they were at least all together again; and it will be intelligible to those whom life has blessed with vicissitude, that Lapham should come home the evening after he had given up everything to his creditors, and should sit down to his supper so cheerful that Penelope could joke in the old way, and tell him that she thought from his looks they had concluded to pay him a hundred cents on every dollar he owed them. (p. 351)

To make the contradictory connection between Lapham's endorsed form of moral heroism and his daughter's disapproved form even clearer, Penelope somewhat earlier claims that it is absolutely wrong to "profit by a wrong" (p. 256). The language of capitalism here and throughout the novel is thus used to support a morality the novel both entirely disapproves as unrealistic in principle even as it clearly approves such extravagant moral sacrifice in practice by enacting it in the fate of the hero. Similarly, when Corey sophistically proposes that Penelope's form of suffering in life may be to be happy "when everyone else is suffering" (p. 355), everyone in the family approves this version of Reverend Sewell's economy of pain, as does the entire novel since the romantic subplot does end happily in the marriage of this unlikely pair. Once again, the business of morality and the morality of business are intertwined in a way the novel both approves and disapproves, even as Lapham heroically refuses himself the escape hatch of such sophistry. Similarly, even though both father and daughter do submit to a trial of spirit, the girl's is clearly presented as suspect, while Lapham's is as clearly presented as exemplary. In sum, *The Rise of Silas Lapham* is a novel radically at odds with itself.

Why is it right for the father to practice a form of excessive moral heroism that it is wrong for his daughter to practice? Why does the novel endorse the father's grim smiles (p. 309) and cruel determination to see another (Rogers) subject himself and so confirm one's superior ethical status, even though it exposes these very same qualities to our critique in his daughter's case as she handles her lover? Shouldn't both forms of extravagant, unrealistic moral heroism be equally disapproved? (The excruciatingly painful nature of the romantic subplot precludes the excuse of comic relief or cautionary edification.) The problem with Michaels's argument, as we can now see, is that he evades this question of the novel's self-contradiction by making equivalent the excessive romanticism of the popular literature of the time and the excessive speculation of the stock market, so that he can also make neatly equivalent as their logical and axiological contraries Howells's restrictive (and quixotic) realism and nostalgic precapitalist (i.e., pre–Gilded Age) ideal of domestic economy. Michaels in this way can rationalize *The Rise of Silas Lapham* for purposes of his critical argument, but only at the expense of its messier and more dramatic aesthetic interest. As we have just seen, however, Howells's realism, which exemplifies itself in the exemplary fate of the novel's protagonist, is actually akin (if not equivalent) to the very excessive romantic ideology of moral heroism it condemns. Similarly, the language of business, of profit and loss, as moralized by the protagonist, is enunciated by his daughter in the service of a romantic ideal of useless sacrifice Howells's realism totally opposes. Why, in short, these formally contradictory relationships?

One answer would be to say that the gender difference, with all its accompanying differences in status, position, and power, defines the difference between the novel's approval and disapproval of the modes of heroic self-denial. It is, after all, morally and aesthetically canonical for a man to practice an excessive form of renunciation, and largely unprecedented for women to do so. In addition, affairs of the heart are not taken as seriously, traditionally speaking, as the worldly affairs of "men at work" – either in war or in business. This answer is too easy, however; for *The Rise of Silas Lapham* portrays all of its major characters as involved in an excessive economy of pain that requires for self-definition forms of self-sacrifice that span the spectrum from relatively petty to sublimely monumental. Consider, for one comic example, how Irene Lapham upbraids her sister for being "such a ninny as to send [Corey] away" on her "account" precisely at the moment when Penelope has decided finally to accept his marriage offer:

> Penelope recoiled from this terrible courage; she did not answer directly, and Irene went on, "Because if you did [send him away for her sake], I'll thank you to bring him back again. I'm not going to have him thinking that I'm dying for a man that never cared for me. It's insulting, and I'm not going to stand it. Now just you send for him!" (p. 358)

Although we are meant to be amused at Irene's "haughty magnanimity" (p. 358), we are also instructed by it. The self in this novel produces itself out of the experience of practicing a stylization of life that entails all forms of renunciation, from the least to the most self-destructive. The genealogy of this practice of the self that I call "smiling through pain" is identified by the narrator only once in the novel, by the by, as it were, in a sentence explaining why Persis Lapham must take upon herself the ultimate – and originary – blame for her husband's ruin. For it is she who first, foremost, and continually forces upon him a memory of guilt and the consequent need for expiation, as far as the Rogers affair is concerned: "She came back to this [explanation for Lapham's fate], with her help-less longing, inbred in all Puritan souls, to have some one specifically suffer for evil in the world, even if it must be herself" (p. 277). Is the novel's formal self-contradiction, therefore, the aesthetic expression of its Puritan heritage, or even of what Geoffrey Galt Harpham has recently termed, after Nietzsche, "the ascetic imperative" that is not only common in Western culture but "common to all culture"?[8]

The problem with this admittedly speculative formulation is that it is a questionable transhistorical explanation that exceeds the necessities of critical argument. Must we really "rise" to the universal level to understand Howells's self-contradicting novel? Clearly not. Must we then perform, on the other hand, as John W. Crowley in *The Black Heart's Truth* does for *A Modern Instance*, an exhaustive psychobiography, "a literary psychology," of the writing of *The Rise of Silas Lapham*?[9] Between minute particulars of the life and times and critical history of all culture, I propose a middle ground of "typical" analysis, in the Weberian style, of the kind of modern soul the characters in the novel are supposed to aspire to realize through their self-imposed sufferings, a process the novel itself performs best via its formal contradiction of being in its own unique way the kind of novel this novel condemns. In short, I propose that *The Rise of Silas Lapham* embodies an ascetic aesthetic not only appropriate to the Puritan origins of the American self, but typical of the post-Enlightenment era.

Harvey Goldman, in *Max Weber and Thomas Mann: Calling and the Shaping of the Self*, presents the best brief description of this type of the ascetic spirit that I am proposing the novel itself most fully realizes, even as all of its characters, especially the Laphams, and most especially Silas Lapham, aspire but fail, by comparison, as fully to realize. (The faded gentility of the Corey family testifies to the superannuated status, the comic irrelevance, of their cultural class in the ethical world of the novel.) I cite now a long but I think useful passage from Goldman on the ascetic "type" of personality:

> In fact, the "type" of the first great entrepreneur is essentially the same as the "type" of the figures who reappear as the politician, scientist, artist, and entrepreneur of Weber's later essays. Aloneness, an inclination to ascetic labor, devoted service to a god, self-denial and systematic self-control, a capacity to resist their own desires as well as the desires, pressures, or temptations of others – these are the qualities all of Weber's *Berufsmenschen* [men of calling] acquire through their submission in the discipline of the calling to an ultimate ideal or goal. The key to their character lies, first, in the subjugation of the "natural" self and second, in its transformation and fortification through the discipline of the calling as a unique relation

of service to their ideal or god: the self is transformed into a personality in a process of formation that shapes it through a calling and equips it for a calling. For the Puritans the life in this calling, carrying out the actions that they believed served their god, became the source of certainty for religious men to combat the uncertainties of death and salvation. For secular men too, according to Weber in his later work, the life in a calling, fitted for the modern situation, holds out the only hope against the threat of purposelessness, directionlessness, and the meaninglessness of death in a civilization now unable to draw on more traditional solutions, dominated as it is by the advance of rationalization.[10]

My point in citing this passage is not simply to allegorize the novel's main character. The qualities, traits, and intentions of the ideal type of the ascetic spirit, of the Protestant ethic, as it relates to rise of capitalism and its later nineteenth-century transformation, do correspond generally, however, to those one finds in Silas Lapham both at the beginning and the end of his career, after he suffers, like Milton's Samson in the mill, the various temptations of a refined and cruelly extravagant life-style that he had aspired to make his own. But I also want to propose a more complicated argument, that the novel itself, in the way I have suggested, embodies this ascetic spirit. Formal, aesthetic contradiction would thus be necessary for the realization of the process of ascetic embodiment. That is, contradiction would be formally intentional in the novel. Nietzsche's *On the Genealogy of Morals* analyzes the law of asceticism precisely in these terms as the endless clash of opposing forces (of will and the body's resistance and inertia). This is what makes possible and defines self-overcoming nature in any ascetic discipline of self-making:

> This secret self-ravishment, this artists' cruelty, this delight in imposing a form upon oneself as a hard, recalcitrant, suffering material and in burning a will, a critique, a contradiction, a contempt, a No into it, this uncanny, dreadfully joyous labor of a soul voluntarily at odds with itself that makes itself suffer out of joy in making suffer – eventually this entire active "bad conscience" – you will have guessed it – as the womb of all ideal and imaginative phenomena, also brought to light an abundance of strange new beauty and affirmation, and perhaps beauty itself. – After all, what would be "beautiful" if the contradiction had not first become conscious of itself, if the ugly had not first said to itself: "I am ugly?"[11]

100

In this light, the smiles of Penelope and her father are as much smiles at their own actively ravishing cruelty against themselves as they are their cruel reactions to the subjection of the Other. In fact, it would be primarily the sign of their own active subjection to a discipline of their own imposition if not making. Such self-subjection, after all, is what Reverend Sewell, who is indeed Howells's spokesman, claims he is so "intensely interested" in at the novel's end: "the moral spectacle which Lapham presented under his changed conditions" (p. 363). (Lapham's ever rougher appearance and manner of dress by novel's end allude to the type of the religious eremite.) What makes *The Rise of Silas Lapham* interesting is the moral spectacle of its own uniquely self-opposing aesthetic condition of having formally to preach against what it must find itself practicing as a novel, a situation that may define the nature of the genre itself.

What I am proposing here, however, is not so much the textualization of the ascetic spirit intimately involved in the rise of capitalism, as what Nietzsche calls "the internalization of man" (p. 84) first carried out by the movement of humankind into cities and recently renewed to an unprecedented degree by modern society. Nietzsche refers by this memorable phrase not only to the turning inward and against ourselves the practices of cruelty originally meant to be performed upon others. He is referring also to their subsequent sublimation into new forms of psychological discipline and defense. Finally, he is also referring to the combined effect of these two developments, to what a Foucaultian critic might call "the internment of human being" in a world where all the prospects of possibility, of infinite horizons, are increasingly withdrawn, blocked, and cut off by an ever-rationalizing world order of the imperial urban centers of a commercial civilization – precisely the world that Michaels argues, unlike Nietzsche or Marx (or Howells, for that matter), we must accept as simply inescapable. Although Nietzsche is of course analyzing explicitly the situation of humankind first in prehistory and then during the originary moments of the Judeo-Christian tradition, his analysis is, I find, perhaps even more pertinent when read as an historically cast critique of his (and still largely our own) present moment.

We can see the specter of this process of internalization and internment, this loss of the possibility of infinitude, of what Words-worth most memorably glosses as "something evermore about to be," not merely negatively in the reduced world of Howells's real-ism (or the even more diminished world of Michaels's naturalism); that is, not merely in what is officially repressed of an excessive, even irrational expenditure. We can also see it operating positively in the ways it principally conditions the major and minor out-comes of the plot. Penelope and Corey, on the one hand, are finally united as part of a package deal. Lapham agrees to let his young West Virginia rivals in the paint business buy him out on two conditions: that he keep control of the production of his deluxe line of paint, the Persis brand (named after his wife); and that Corey be taken into their newly expanded business as a partner (something he had always refused to do), so that Corey can finally put into practice his plans for the paint business in Mexico. Appar-ently, then, thanks to this threat of imminent departure, all the formerly embarrassing moral and social wrinkles are suddenly ironed out. For Penelope now accepts his latest proposal. On the other hand, even the marginal utopian venture of the English aristocrats that causes Lapham so much moral anguish and en-ables his rise in moral stature, is also intricately intertwined, as we have seen, with the torturous schemes of various entrepreneurs. In short, the ground of experience in the novel is wholly conditioned by the imperialistic economic order that is necessarily defined by the growing rationalization of the world and consequent diminish-ment of the sense of the infinite. (Such "conditioning," of course, does not mean determination, whether of a reductively materialist or textual kind.)

By sense of the infinite I mean what Kant in *The Critique of Judgement* analyzes as the sublime. For Kant, the sublime is that paradoxical experience in which the individual imagination reads its failure to represent in definite images some boundless totality like mountainous abysses or creative genius as the sign of the human mind's power to constitute via its abstract ideas the realm of experience itself: "For the imagination, although it finds noth-ing beyond the sensible to which it can attach itself, yet feels itself unbounded by this removal of its limitations; and thus that very abstraction [from such limitations] is a[n indeterminate] presentation of the Infinite, which can be nothing but a mere negative presentation, but which yet expands the soul."[12] The sublime's negative transcendence of experience Kant compares to the highest command of the Jewish law: "Perhaps there is no sublimer passage . . . than the command, 'Thou shalt not make to thyself any graven image, nor likeness of anything which is in heaven or in the earth or under the earth'."[13] The sublime experience thus realizes in the modern context the iconoclastic ascetic imperative of the Judeo-Christian tradition. A sublime aesthetic, therefore, necessarily depends upon texts of self-transcending images, upon an imagination that is radically and intentionally at odds with itself. And in a world where the experience of the sublime is increasingly rationalized out of existence, just as Michaels rationalized away the sublimely conflicted nature of Howells's novel, the only place where the ascetic spirit can practice and realize the sublime imagination is such self-opposing texts, which are the sites for our modern self-opposing culture to reveal itself.

Foucault in "What Is Enlightenment?" provides a useful gloss on what I am reaching for. He focuses there on Kant and Baudelaire as defining figures of our "modernity," which he finds necessarily entails an "ironic heroization of the present" involving an "ascetic elaboration of the self" in the "different place" of art. Modernity, for Foucault, is thus primarily "an attitude, an ethos, a philosophical life in which the critique of what we are is at one and the same time the historical analysis of the limits that are imposed on us and an experiment with the possibility of going beyond them."[14] In terms of my argument, then, *The Rise of Silas Lapham* would be the place where the emerging culture of speculative capitalism suffers an ascesis in the exemplary fate of its hero as sublimely embodied by this self-opposing text. An immanent critique, a negative transcendence, enacts itself here in an ascetic transgression of the aesthetic limits of a novel that condemns itself as sublimely as its finally antiheroic hero does himself, as the narrator reports:

> All those who were concerned in his affairs said he behaved well, and even more than well, when it came to the worst. The prudence, the good sense, which he had shown in the first years of his success, and of which great prosperity seemed to have bereft him, came

back; and these qualities used in his own behalf, commended him as much to his creditors as the anxiety he showed that no one should suffer by him; this even made some of them doubtful of his sincerity. . . . He saw that it was useless to try to go on in the old way, and he preferred to go back and begin the world anew, in the hills at Lapham. He put the house at Kankeen Square, with everything else he had, into the payment of his debts, and Mrs. Lapham found it easier to leave it for the old farmstead in Vermont [than she had thought she would]. . . . This thing and that is embittered to us, so that we may be willing to relinquish it; the world, life itself, is embittered to most of us, so that we are glad to have done with them at last; and this home was haunted with such memories to each of those who abandoned it that to go was less exile than escape. . . . He was returning to begin life anew . . . (pp. 352–3)

Lapham's final words to Reverend Sewell put in homelier fashion than the narrator's do what the nature of this "less exile than escape," this sublimely negative transcendence of our self-opposing culture, is really most like: "'About what I done? Well, it don't always seem as if I done it,' replied Lapham. 'Seems sometimes as if it was hole opened for me, and I crept out of it. I don't know,' he added thoughtfully, biting the corner of his stiff mustache – 'I don't know as I should always say it paid; but if I done it, and the thing was to do over again, right in the same way, I guess I should have to do it'" (p. 365). If Kant is right that the most sublime passage of the Old Law is the prohibition of graven images, then the most sublime passage of the New Law must be the scriptural archetype of Lapham's striking, down-to-earth commonplace: "He is risen."

NOTES

1. W. D. Howells, *The Rise of Silas Lapham,* eds. W. J. Meserve and David J. Nordloh (Bloomington: Indiana University Press, 1971); all citations are from the Viking Penguin photo-offset reproduction of this text (New York: Viking Penguin, 1983).
2. Walter Benn Michaels, *The Gold Standard and the Logic of Naturalism: American Literature at the Turn of the Century* (Berkeley: University of California Press, 1987), p. 41.
3. Ibid., p. 41.

4. Ibid., p. 28.
5. Ibid., p. 28.
6. Ibid., p. 41.
7. Ibid., p. 178.
8. Geoffrey Galt Harpham, *The Ascetic Imperative in Culture and Criticism* (Chicago: University of Chicago Press, 1987), p. xi.
9. John W. Crowley, *The Black Heart's Truth: The Early Career of W. D. Howells* (Chapel Hill: University of North Carolina Press, 1985), p. x.
10. Harvey Goldman, *Max Weber and Thomas Mann: Calling and the Shaping of the Self* (Berkeley: University of California Press, 1988), p. 19.
11. Friedrich Nietzsche, *On the Genealogy of Morals*, trans. Walter Kaufman and R. J. Hollingdale, in *On the Genealogy of Morals and Ecce Homo*, ed. Walter Kaufman (New York: Vintage, 1969), pp. 87–8.
12. Immanuel Kant, *The Critique of Judgement*, trans. J. H. Bernhard (New York: Hafner Press, 1951), p. 115.
13. Ibid.
14. Michel Foucault, "What Is Enlightenment?" in *The Foucault Reader*, ed. Paul Rabinow (New York: Pantheon Books, 1984), pp. 42, 50.

6

The Rise of Silas Lapham: The Business of Morals and Manners

JAMES M. COX

*T*HE *Rise of Silas Lapham* has always been and surely will continue to be William Dean Howells's most available work, the work that connects him to the larger world of readers. There are of course other Howells novels that will be candidates for the position. Some will claim the earlier *A Modern Instance* as the essential Howells; others will find in the later *A Hazard of New Fortunes* a gravity of social consciousness that gives the novel a weight lacking in the earlier work. In light of Howells's voluminous production, minority candidates will inevitably be advanced. Some few will opt for *Annie Kilburn* or *The Minister's Charge;* and there will no doubt be a few who enter pleas for *The Son of Royal Langbrith* or *The Landlord at Lion's Head.* Then too there will be advocates for *Indian Summer* as evidence that Howells could hold his own with James in the international scene. Lionel Trilling went so far as to single out *The Vacation of the Kelwyns* as an example of his resilient strength. Yet anyone reflecting upon Howells's fate knows that none of these minority candidates – not even *A Modern Instance* or *A Hazard of New Fortunes* – will ever challenge the preeminence of *The Rise of Silas Lapham.*

There was a time, even in my memory, when *The Rise of Silas Lapham* was standard reading in the high schools of the land. It represented American literature in novel form just as *Silas Marner* represented English literature. But that day is long since past. Preparing to write on *Lapham*, I ventured into the county library of my native Grayson County, Virginia, to see what Howells might be there only to discover that not a single volume – not even *Lapham* – was to be found. Standing alone in that knowledge, I half realized that none of Howells's works will in all probability experience

a revival. Yet feeling the defensiveness so common to rural South-
erners, I attributed the absence of Howells to the general lack of
literary culture in my county. Imagine my surprise then, tinged
with a certain pleasure, when, a month later, I pursued my search
for Howells holdings in Norwich, Vermont, now supposed to be
the richest township in the state, and found not a single volume of
Howells in that library. To be sure, Norwich residents can go to the
Dartmouth College library only a mile away and find Howells to
their hearts' desire. Still, the absence of Howells in such a literate
town as Norwich was glaringly substantial. After all, Silas Lapham
is one of two famous fictional characters who hail from Vermont;
Simon Legree is the other. Needless to say *Uncle Tom's Cabin* was
prominently present in the Norwich library, though precious few
Norwich residents would wish to remember, if they ever knew,
that Legree was their compatriot.

To see the absence of Howells is to want to think that his demise
is more recent than it is, but it had actually begun well before the
bitter attack on him by Mencken and Sinclair Lewis in the twenties. When, in 1911, Harper decided to bring out a uniform edition
of his work, the project foundered after only six volumes were
published. What a fine irony for American letters that Edmund
Wilson, more than half a century later, should greet the Center for
Editions of American Authors edition of *Their Wedding Journey*,
which inaugurated the complete edition of Howells's works, as the
preposterous fruits of the MLA. Not that Wilson utterly despised
Howells. His later letters reflect a moderate appreciation of *A Hazard of New Fortunes*, yet Wilson, coming to full stature in the twenties as he did, could hardly help seeing the Dean as a withered
branch.

It is not only the twenties that left Howells enthusiasts (if such
truly exist) perpetually on the defensive. The academic canoniza-
tion of Mark Twain and Henry James put Howells forever in a
disadvantaged position between them. It was the same position he
occupied in life as the brilliant editor – but editor nonetheless –
who had recognized their genius and sought their work for his
magazine. If he outlived both of them in life it was but a sign that
he had lived too long. Years before he died he wrote Henry James
that he was "comparatively a dead cult with his statues cut down

and the grass growing over them in the pale moonlight." That was the same Henry James who had, in the wake of the neglect that greeted *The Princess Casamassima*, nonetheless contended, in a letter to Howells, that his works would one day kick over their gravestones and dance into life. James had, in an "open letter" to be read on Howells's seventy-fifth birthday, affectionately concluded, "Your really beautiful time will come." Forty years later, Lional Trilling, the only critic of major cultural status to take on the task of reclaiming Howells, ended his essay by quoting James and ruefully wondering whether, in the wake of World War II, when extremes of consciousness and their attendant violent visions had become the commonplace, Howells, who so assiduously cultivates the moderate sentiments, would ever experience the abundance of critical attention devoted to James and Mark Twain. Now, almost forty more years since Trilling made his rear guard effort on Howells's behalf, the beautiful time seems as far away as ever.

Yet anyone who has read *The Rise of Silas Lapham* knows that Trilling was right in contending, however defensively, for some recognition of Howells. He saw the stubborn persistence Howells brought to the novel form, saw the stolidity as well as the adroitness of Howells's particular strategies of representing the daily issue of middle class life. Thus, according the Trilling, when Basil March spends chapters at the outset of *A Hazard of New Fortunes* hunting a house, his search cannot properly be seen by some interpretive enthusiast as symbolic of some vastly larger quest. It is instead, observes Trilling, simply a house hunt. And he goes on to insist that the increasing inability of our present culture to find interest or meaning or pleasure in the ordinary is precisely what drives us to desire violent and passionate action on the one hand or to overburden the literal with symbolic meaning on the other.

Trilling's effort to shield Howells was in one way the tribute of a fine and sensitive critic to a writer he felt was strong enough to deserve recognition. At the same time, Trilling remained just dubious enough of Howells's achievement to concentrate his criticism as much on the weakness of the culture neglecting Howells as on Howells's imaginative strengths. Thus when he observed that Basil March's search for a house is just what it purports to be — a house hunt — he might at least have wondered about the house of

Silas Lapham. Indeed, Howells's clear determination to make Lapham's house stand for more than a house not only threatens his project of representing the merely ordinary but involves him in woodenly symbolizing it to serve his plot. Without wishing to press the point, I think it significant that Trilling's extensive essay never once refers to *The Rise of Silas Lapham.*

The best way to gain a perspective on the book – and, I might add, to Howells's lifelong fictional project – is to place it between the work of Mark Twain and Henry James. To so place it is to see Howells not only where he saw himself but also where we encounter him today. The novels of James and Mark Twain that shed the best light on *Lapham* are *The American* and *Adventures of Huckleberry Finn.* Some might feel that *The Bostonians* would be a better choice, particularly in light of the fact that it accompanied *Lapham* and *Huckleberry Finn* in serial publication in the *Century* magazine in 1885. Certainly all those novels reflect, twenty years after Appomattox, an effort of imaginative reconciliation between North and South. Yet if we pursued that thematic action we should certainly want to see Henry Adams's *Democracy* as the forerunner of them all. No, *The American* is altogether more appropriate. It was the novel that Howells had persuaded James to divert from publication elsewhere and give to him for serialization in *The Atlantic.*

The relation of Silas Lapham to Christopher Newman and Huck Finn should be almost glaringly apparent, for he is at once a businessman and a vernacular character. To be sure, he doesn't take over his narrative in the manner of Huck Finn, yet just as clearly Howells does not wish to reduce him to a mere dialect character, as is evident by his observation that Lapham pronounces *coat* as "cut" and *road* as "rud" – this after he has just transcribed Lapham's speech – as if to remind his readers that the transcription is by no means an attempt to render the full dialect. Indeed there has always been a sense among cultivated readers of dialect that Lapham, in his swagger as well as in his speech rhythms, actually seems more Western than Northeastern.

But the kinship of Lapham to Newman and Huck Finn does not end with vocation and vernacular. He shares with Newman both a business confidence and a cultural innocence. His whole situation is remarkably similar to Newman's, for he is caught at the precise moment when the business success that has given him confidence is catapulting him into the confrontation with the Coreys, whose cultural security, like that of the Bellegardes, rests not upon money but upon manners. Manners are, for the Coreys as well as the Bellegardes, the *possession* of social power through a sufficient number of generations to give the descendent social bearing. This passage through generations is precisely the inheritance that gives a family the individuality of identity coupled with presence inside an exclusive society. The chief difference between the Bellegardes and the Coreys is that the Bellegardes' identity rests on blood lines; thus authority as well as real power remains in the hands of the parents, who can dictate their daughters' marriages. Then too, the issue of illegitimacy becomes a shadow line in societies and families who rely on blood purity for identity. Realistic novelists like James who became involved in such a society were always open to the seduction of such a shadow line, pursuit of which took them into secret assignations and gothic romance. Newman himself is drawn into such a plot as he pursues Mrs. Bread and secures his evidence of a family secret – evidence with which he intends to revenge himself upon the Bellegardes, who have exercised their absolute and arbitrary authority over their daughter, forbidding her marriage to Newman after at first authorizing it. It is Newman's ultimate renunciation of this plotted revenge that brings him back to his authentic good nature – the good nature that had, at the outset of the novel, renounced his intended revenge on a business rival. That initial renunciation was part and parcel of his visionary determination to launch himself into his European adventure.

The Coreys' superiority to Lapham rests on much less secure grounds than that of the Bellegardes. Their "line" is of much more recent origins; their society, rooted in theories of equality rather than in divisions of class, survives on class distinctions rather than divisions. Lacking the authority to forbid their son to marry "beneath" him, they are reduced to the weak hope that he will somehow have the "good breeding" to marry someone of his own type. Given such insecure authority, the Coreys, as well as the Laphams "beneath" them, live on lines of inhibition and anxiety. They themselves are only one generation removed from aggressive com-

mercial interests that secured them the leisure to cultivate themselves; their aversion to the vulgarity of business thus contains an
element of self-repression.

Finally there is the issue of art that runs like a blade through
both novels. Both Newman and Lapham display a remarkable
naïveté about the nature of art. Neither sees the difference between
a copy and an original precisely because both men are themselves
sufficiently original to feel that all paintings are merely copies that
can in turn be copied and acquired. Confident of themselves, they
are sure that the reality of their world takes precedence over art,
which at best can decorate their lives as possessions. Faced with
these two originals, the ostensible custodians of culture – the Bellegardes and the Coreys – fail to *appreciate* their value. If Lapham's
originality is in his crude yet sturdy nature, Newman's rests in his
good nature, his generous yet egocentric radiation of innocence,
confidence, and well-being. Lapham's relation to art is reflected in
his occupation and preoccupation with paint itself. He presides
over the first stage in its refinement from its mineral ore to the
possibilities of color. If his mineral paint mine is rooted in local
color, Lapham goes beyond dialect to general color; he stands in
stark contrast to Bromfield Corey, who has passed through the
leisured cultivation of culture (on his father's commercial capital)
to become an amateur painter. Newman's confident innocence,
grounded on his self-made capital, enables him to take his ease in
the Louvre, sure that all original paintings are after all only copies
of nature. That is why he makes little distinction between a copy
and an original.

To touch on Newman's innocence is to face his deepest difference from Lapham. Lapham is himself innocent in an ultimate
sense. He has done no one any great wrong in the past; he has
made his money honestly; he has treated the world fairly; he has a
generous heart and he is a good family man. The only blemish on
his record is his (and his wife's) knowledge that, after having a
partner whose capital he used to expand his business, he crowded
that partner out of the business when commercial opportunity
afforded such aggression. Yet that blemish is his tender spot, so
tender that his wife can irritate it at will. Their relationship, though
faithful in the extreme, is nonetheless touched with dis-ease. Both

112

of them, particularly Mrs. Lapham, cultivate their consciences to the point of hypersensitivity. Whatever is erotic in their marriage (and there is something since they do have children) is being channeled along lines of financial and moral profit. Love itself becomes the major inhibition. Small wonder that Silas thinks first of hiring young Corey and "making a man" of him; there *is* the erotic manifesting itself even as Lapham denies that he has an interest in promoting a marriage between one of his daughters and the Corey family. Small wonder too that both the Lapham parents misread young Corey's intentions, believing him to be in love with the conventional beauty, Irene. But then the Coreys misread the relationship on exactly the same lines. And in each case it is the wife, not the husband, who takes the lead in the misjudgment; after all, love is their "province," and they think about it first and last, yet they are helpless to do anything about it. They can talk about it with neither their husbands nor their children. The whole subject is but one more inhibition forming the tyrannical region of the conscience. It is just this gnawing conscience that relates the world of the Laphams to that of Huckleberry Finn, who, as innocent as Lapham, is dogged by a bad conscience no matter what course of action he chooses. Yet for all Huck's problems with his conscience, he is a far cry from Lapham's condition. The fact that he has his boyhood being in the old slave society of the South not only shields him from our criticism; it makes us convert what seem to him sins into acts of moral heroism. Never mind that there is always an element of self-interest in Huck; never mind that Huck is neither as generous nor is his friend Jim as selfless as a postslavery audience is determined to see them on their raft; never mind that the drift of the great river itself is carrying them ever deeper into slavery. After all, the river, obeying a law of nature, is not responsible for the slavery in its lower reaches; Huck is but a boy in helpless flight from his drunken father; Jim is a fugitive slave trying to avoid being sold down the river. All are remarkably free of moral responsibility for their action. Their "freedom" comes at the expense of the historically invalidated society which, twenty years after Appomattox, is being morally indicted for the chattel slavery at its center. That essential exchange leaves a surplus of good feeling and self-gratulation for the post–Civil War readers of which we today are as securely members as were Mark Twain's readers in 1885.

The ultimate form of the exchange is, of course the language of *Huckleberry Finn*. By removing himself as writer and in effect turning the whole book over to Huck's deviant vernacular, Mark Twain at once participated in the irresponsibility so central to his whole imaginative endeavor, yet remained fully generous to his character. Deviantly negative in its structure and played off against an absent yet implicitly present "correct" structured language of formal rules, Huck's vernacular, for all its presence in a world of slavery, represents for its readers a recovery of the illusory freedom that has been lost in the exchange of childhood for adulthood. Surely it is the adult reader's remarkable gain – the recovery of childhood's freedom without loss of the national good feeling resulting from the nation's march from the slavery of its childhood to the freedom of its maturity – that is threatened by the ending of the book. Small wonder that both Jim and Huck are inevitably exempted from criticism of their action, and the responsibility for the failed ending falls upon Tom Sawyer and Mark Twain – as if it couldn't be part of Huck's character either to tell his story in such a way that the blame *would* fall on Tom Sawyer.

To see, even in such a rudimentary way, how Mark Twain's act and form work is to gain a telling perspective on *The Rise of Silas Lapham*. If Mark Twain had brought Huck Finn on stage for a second appearance, Howells does the same with Bartley Hubbard. But whereas Huck moves from the position of supporting actor in *The Adventures of Tom Sawyer* to become the hero of his own narrative, Bartley Hubbard descends from his role of central character in *A Modern Instance* to perform the function of introducing Silas Lapham. The fact that Bartley is a newspaper reporter is of great importance to Howells's form since Howells's narration is itself reportorial. Unlike James, who, in *The American*, moved his narrative observer into intimate quarters with his hero Christopher Newman and largely confined him there, where he indulgently elaborates as well as pursues Newman's consciousness, Howells keeps his narration at a level of detachment from all his characters. Though he retains in a technical sense the omniscient narrator, Howells reduces him to the role of reporting rather than overseeing. This does not mean that the narrator is without judgment. He is actually quite full of it, but the judgment is, or seems to be, directed toward objectifying both society and characters. Narration thus features extended dialogue accompanied by compressed stage and scene directions. Talk in a Howells novel takes precedence over action and even rivals description.

What Howells's narration comes down to is a system of subtraction. We begin with Bartley Hubbard interviewing Lapham for the purpose of writing a feature article in which the ostensible aim is to inflate Lapham's value while the journalist's ironic eye designs covertly to expose the vulgarity of the mineral paint king. If we look at Bartley as surplus value brought from a prior Howells novel in order to perform the work of introducing a new character, we are close to the dynamics of the book. Bartley is, after all, the writer as journalist. Not only is he writing about a businessman; writing is his business. Though he has less money than Lapham, he feels that he has more class. We are even told, in one of those compressed observations so characteristic of Howells's detached narration, that Bartley's affable indulgence of Lapham's volubility concealed his inward derision of his subject. He is in the business of extracting from Lapham's crude vernacular his feature story for his "Solid Men of Boston" series in much the same way that Lapham has extracted his mineral paint from nature. What is most important in this exchange is that Bartley's finished story will in effect cover up Lapham's crude vernacular just as effectively as Lapham's refined mineral paint covers up natural defects and even nature itself. Bartley's finished product will present Lapham as a "solid man" of Boston. And here Howells is particularly careful to give samples of Bartley's finished journalistic product to show just how he has "painted" his subject.

To see this writing "business" is to begin to see Howells's own method. Bartley gains profit as a writer by writing quickly and covering up his perceived crudity of his subject at the same time he conceals his own feelings of superiority that take the form of suppressed derision of Lapham. It is clear, moreover, that Bartley's feelings of superiority rest on his linguistic capacity to "order" his subject, first by seducing Lapham into a self-publicizing narrative and then by retailing – and even retelling – the narrative to conform to the conventions of a saleable and packaged commodity. Beyond that, Lapham, the subject, is in an uneasy collaboration with his "biographer." Always at the edge of awareness that Bartley may secretly be mocking him, he yet cannot resist his "natural" faith in himself and his paint.

This then is the social situation and dramatic scene with which Howells introduces his novel. Using an old character to introduce a new one, Howells engages in a double capitalization of Bartley that actually creates surplus value for the author. Beyond that, it confers on readers who know *A Modern Instance* a privileged feeling of inherited cultural wealth not unlike that enjoyed by the Coreys in the novel. Whereas Bartley's newspaper story about Lapham conceals Lapham's vernacular, Howells's narrative features it — and features it in such a way that it reflects Lapham's essential innocence of spirit yet exposes a certain social crudity of bearing in the central figure of the novel. Howells's representation of Lapham's vernacular provides ground on which social distinctions are made. It is in effect the base (in every sense of the word) language of the novel. Even Bartley regrets that the conventions of journalism prevent him from using Lapham's own words in making his portrait.

If Howells's narration, by featuring Lapham's vernacular, exposes his crudity, it implies a certain moral strength of character. The implication is based as much on the negative exposure of Bartley as on any positive evidence in Lapham's language. Bartley's character — essentially shallow, cynical, sensual, and irreverent — is reflected in his facile account of Lapham's life. By virtue of Howells's fiction, Bartley's interview with Lapham comes early in the span of life depicted in *A Modern Instance*, granting "regular" Howells readers the privilege of already knowing Bartley's bad end, which is here represented as an unknown future. Since Bartley is discarded (so much for surplus value!) after the initial chapter, his moral weakness has only the dramatic value of implying a contrasting strength in Lapham that Howells has neither to insist on nor to demonstrate.

The great strength of this opening encounter, beyond its fine economy of introducing Lapham, lies in its exposure of the essential dis-ease suffered by characters in what is theoretically a classless society yet is both actually and relentlessly a middle class society. Members of such a class seek the means literally to "move up" in the society. Since there is neither an aristocracy above nor a peasantry below, the upward mobility is directed toward the acquisition of culture. Culture, in this social sense, is the refinement that may give grace to the natural man. The middle class wish would always be that this grace is somehow inborn, a quality that "money can't buy." To possess it is to be a member of what Huck Finn calls "the quality." Yet the Gilded Age, the age of Mark Twain, James, and Howells, was precisely the period when rampant capitalism made acquisition of such culture possible on a large scale. James himself, in *The American Scene*, ruefully remarked the sad change that overtook Newport, Rhode Island, after the Civil War, when the "tasteful scale" of the prewar town was overtaken by the garish mansions (scathingly denominated "white elephants") erected by tycoons.

The drama residing in the pressure of upward mobility is what exercises Howells's imagination. It is fully in evidence in the prelude between Bartley and Lapham. Just as Lapham with his unbuttoned vernacular is Howells's major creative contribution to the novel, the anxiety attending that vernacular reflects Howells's sure grasp of the psychology involved in negotiating the social distinctions erected within the middle class. We are no sooner into the scene between Bartley and Lapham than we see Lapham's disease, which is absolutely related to Bartley's easy familiarity. With his seemingly "natural" language and his success as a "solid man" of Boston, Lapham ought to be the one at ease, yet he is apprehensive of danger, suspecting Bartley's irony and sensing the loss of his individuality to the process of being packaged in the hard convention of the success story.

Even more interesting is the *narration's* relation to the conversation and gestures between the two men. First there is the moment when, after all but boasting of the high quality of both his wife and his paint, Lapham tells of advertising his paint all over the landscape — on fences, bridges, walls, barns, and rocks. Then,

> Bartley had taken his seat on the window-sill, and Lapham, standing before him, now put his huge foot close to Bartley's thigh; neither of them minded that. (p. 14)

That final independent clause implies a whole social world even as it remains "straight" reporting. It at once discloses a careless intimacy between Bartley and Lapham at the same time it suggests a sufficiently decorous and restrained social world where such casual intimacy would indeed be "minded." This does not mean that the narrative disapproves of Bartley and Lapham; it does mean that such gestures are characteristic of a lower and not a higher social order. Two pages later another such incident occurs. Having told Bartley of his having enlisted in the Union army at the time of the Civil War, Lapham says

> "So I went. I got through; and you can call me Colonel, if you want to. Feel there!" Lapham took Bartley's thumb and forefinger and put them on a bunch in his leg, just above the knee. "Any thing hard?"
>   "Ball?"
>   Lapham nodded. "Gettysburg. That's my thermometer. If it wa'n't for that, I shouldn't know when to come in when it rains."
>   (p. 16)

Lapham's uninhibited willingness to have Bartley touch him merely affirms the existence of a social order inhibited precisely along these lines. Indeed, it is a tribute to Howells's strength that the counterthrust of this implied inhibition actually reaches across a hundred years to touch a modern reader who could hardly fail to be struck by the sexual innuendo emerging almost embarrassingly right through the dialogue.

I stress this moment because it touches (surely the right word) the emotional dynamics as well as the very substance of Howells's plot. The plot of the novel, as everyone knows, is doubly hinged. There is the Lapham family's entry into the society of the Coreys, and there is Lapham's overextension in business that leads to his demise. The encounter with the Coreys rests primarily on manners and is directly in line with the emotional stress that is evident in Lapham's interview with Bartley. The climax of the encounter is of course the dinner party at the Coreys. The overextension in business leads to Lapham's failure, but his conduct throughout his decline is sufficiently exemplary that, in terms of this plot, he gains in moral stature as he loses his financial base. Thus the title of the book has its own neat irony: Lapham is morally falling as he is rising financially, and morally rising as he is financially falling. In terms of this plot, the crucial scene, I suppose, would be the burning of the Laphams' new house, since this large, unfinished structure signals both a large investment and a move into a more lavish, if newer, Boston residential area.

There is good reason for my uncertainty. The burning of the house comes from Lapham's own careless hands; though he did not intentionally set the fire he nonetheless has cause to burn it since his psychic involvement in it goes beyond its money value. In a very real sense, he would rather see it burn than see it sold to raise needed capital to save his failing fortunes. The house is for Lapham not so much the sign of his success as it is the expansive embodiment of his upward social mobility. His relation to the house is thus but further evidence that the emotional center of the novel lies not in Lapham's business but in his advance upon the social world above him. The profit of his business *is* the very house he is building; small wonder that his investment in it threatens to go beyond interest into the principal.

All of which brings us back to the dominance of what we may call social reality over private morality. Admittedly this dominance is not asserted in the novel; indeed the obverse, if anything, is true. We hear much about the conscience in the book, and a very bad conscience it is. Mrs. Lapham is the primary agent assigned to keep her finger, as if it were a lancet, on the tender spot, harking ever back to the moment Lapham crowded out the partner who had helped provide the capital for his expansion from what we well could call the "local color" paint business into the national and even the international market. Yet the whole line of logic that runs through Mrs. Lapham's harping (and it shouldn't be forgotten that she originally urged Lapham to go into the partnership) on to Lapham's subsequent response of helping his erstwhile partner Rogers and ending in the disastrous chain of events that follow upon that liaison – this line of logic is actually quite wooden. More important, there is a troubling, because mechanical, relation between money and morals in this whole plot line. It amounts to Howells's setting out to subtract Lapham's money from him in order to supply credit to his moral bank account, and it has a manufactured cast about it. The house burns just after the insurance has lapsed; the Rogers connection leads the hitherto stolid and "solid" Lapham to begin speculating and to neglect his paint, all of which incapacitates him from meeting the West Virginia competition. We never really see this competition in the form of real characters. Finally there are the unlikely Englishmen – possible frauds produced by the redoubtable Rogers – who are naive enough to buy out Lapham's failing business and save him until he determines to tell them the truth about his weak competitive position. His honest behavior with the West Virginians so impresses Charles Bellingham, brother of Mrs. Corey and rock of proper Bostonian probity, that he affirms Lapham's behavior to be that of a gentleman. And so Lapham redeemed is Lapham broken as well as broke. He returns, with his vernacular, to the Vermont homestead whence he came and, presumably where he belongs.

This is essentially the redemptive plot of the book, giving it a symmetry signifying the just balance between morals and money. Merely to rehearse the sequence is to be reminded of its essential lack of drama. None of the participants – the West Virginians, the Englishmen, or Bellingham – are really fleshed out. As a result, Lapham, far from moving on lines of free will, as his author would have us believe, is actually on a forced march rather ruthlessly arranged by his author. This march may balance the books in a technical way, yet it seems most to remind us that what we may call the real business of the book is in the other plot, the plot leading to the Coreys' dinner party for the Laphams, surely the most memorable scene in the book.

The strength of the scene and the strength of the narrative that has led up to that scene lies in Howells's sure grasp of the emotions involved, central of which is the emotion of embarrassment. Embarrassment in this novel is the emotion of defensive self-consciousness felt by people of social inexperience at the threshold of crossing into the exclusive area of the socially experienced. True social experience is cultural wealth, which is to say the possession of sufficient cultural capital to be at ease in the coded manners of what we call society. The Lapham family, for all their financial wealth, are culturally impoverished. The more they advance into high culture the more culturally poor they feel. As head of the family, Lapham possesses the greatest potentiality for embarrassment precisely because of his seemingly uninhibited language. Howells's strength in this novel is to have seized on the contradiction between Lapham's overt, headlong, and even headstrong vernacular and his covert insecurity, and to have kept forcing Lapham toward the crisis with the Coreys.

It is just this contradiction that characterizes not only Lapham but the entire Lapham family, with the possible exception of Irene. They tell themselves that they do not want to be in the Corey world, yet they do; that they are as good as the Coreys, yet they are beset with doubts; that they are satisfied with their lot in life, yet they aren't. They are, moreover, often exposing this common trait in their dealings with each other. Thus Mrs. Lapham takes pleasure in twitting Lapham about this covert eagerness to rise beyond his stature by getting in with the Coreys and possibly achieving a marriage of his daughter to Tom Corey. Much of Penelope's humor comes from her droll recognition of her father's spreading his feathers in order to impress his betters. Even Mrs. Lapham's persistent harping on Lapham's bad conscience concerning Rogers draws its force from his repeated insistence that he has nothing to hide.

What is important is the manner in which Howells makes this state of affairs clear. In the main it is accomplished by means of dialogue followed by compact authorial innuendo. The reason that the two older Laphams are more vulnerable to such analytic exposure is that their speech falls clearly into the category of countrified vernacular. Lapham's speech is characterized by a careless, even reckless, self-confidence – the seeming assurance, bluntness, and impatience of a man of action. As for Mrs. Lapham, instead of expressing desire in the form of a wish ("I wish you would . . .") she habitually says, "I want you should . . .," as if she were perennially in the position of desiring a moral imperative. However much their country talk signals their essential honesty, unpretentiousness, and natural simplicity, it still fixes them at a position of social disadvantage in the world of the novel. As long as they speak as they do (and Howells makes no modifications of their speech during the novel), they must perforce feel their insecurity, since they are, in effect, away from home in their speech. Significantly, the Lapham children do not talk like their parents but are already on the generational escalator of upward mobility. If they were confined to the vernacular of their parents, young Tom Corey could not, in the manners that ultimately govern the world of this novel, consider marrying either one of them. Penelope, the one he does marry, has already advanced to the sophistication of being able to mimic her father. Even more important, Penelope reads books – books that are clearly literature. Knowledge of literature is the chief possession that marks the distinction between the world of the Coreys and that of the Laphams. If Penelope's knowledge of George Eliot and Dickens forms the basis of her converse with Tom Corey, her drollery secures her from the embarrassment that forever threatens Irene in her encounters.

Embarrassment literally colors the relation of the Laphams to the Coreys. Grounded on their insecurity and inhibition, it is everywhere potentially present. Thus Irene blushes when she sees Tom; she even colors when she shows him where the girls' bedrooms will be in the new house. Lapham's strongly asserted views on architecture begin to disintegrate in the face of the architect's easy presentation of the principles of good taste in home construction. All Silas can do is to adopt these new attitudes as if they were his own and proceed to instruct those less knowledgeable than he in these matters. For all his bluster about being equal to the Coreys, his insecurity is painfully evident. Finally, Penelope's courtship with Tom is tormented with embarrassment. We could put it almost as a law that, in the actual sequence of the book, social insecurity at once precedes and brings on financial insecurity. That is why the dinner at the Coreys' is the crucial as well as the unforgettable scene in the novel. It is also why the narration, at that moment, focuses on Lapham's consciousness with a rigor almost Jamesian.

It is, after all, the moment toward which the emotional weight of the narrative has been gravitating. True to both the tone and action of the book, this crisis literally turns on embarrassment. Lapham, initially brimming with confidence at the idea of a dinner with the Coreys, is increasingly disconcerted as actual preparations for the dinner are undertaken. Arriving at the Coreys' dressed in formal attire for the first time in his life, not knowing whether to put on or take off his gloves upon entering the Corey portals, looking around both desperately and furtively to find out just what to do as the dinner begins, and finally being sandbagged into drinking wine because he is too ashamed to ask for water, Lapham – who never has "wine at table" – regresses from his state of silent and desperate repression into his natural character of uninhibited expression. Since Lapham slightly drunk and expressive is no longer embarrassed, the embarrassment is transferred to the reader. The transfer is the surest sign of Howells's strength as a writer. No wonder Mark Twain responded to Howells's mastery in such moments to the extent of feeling that *he* was the person being portrayed (as indeed he might have been in this instance). It is precisely in this moment when Lapham loses his self-consciousness that the reader feels sympathy – even empathy – for him. We might even say that the reader's embarrassment for as well as by Lapham is a reflection of Howells's recognition that embarrassment is a central emotion of middle class social existence. Who of us has not had a searing experience similar to Lapham's in whatever upward mobility we have managed to negotiate?

Our embarrassment for Lapham marks the beginning of the process of "redemption" that Howells's moral plot is at the threshold of executing. The action begins the next day when Lapham acknowledges utter defeat and delivers himself of a shameful, because shameless, apology to young Tom Corey. Confessing himself unworthy to be in the company of Corey, Lapham sinks to the point of helplessly asking whether his conduct caused talk about him after he left the party, to which Corey replies that Lapham has been among *gentlemen* whose behavior is superior to talking over the lapses of guests. Corey can only view Lapham's abject response with an aversion bordering on disgust.

Howells's narrative strategy in this sequence significantly denies access to Lapham's inner consciousness between the time of his drunkenness and the moment of his abject apology to Corey. In other words, we do not see Lapham's reflective process even at this critical moment (and we do not see it during the novel other than when he is struggling to remain engaged in the dinner-table and after-dinner conversation). Yet when Corey leaves Lapham in disgust, we are allowed to see his own reflections in ample measure, beginning with his disgust and revolving full circle beyond self-judgment to recognition that Lapham himself may have been the superior figure in the entire sequence. The implications of this narrative deployment are evident. Lapham's language *is* his consciousness; it at once defines and completes him as an object for social interaction and observation. Though he is not explicitly denied an inner or private consciousness, he is all the same largely confined to his language and generalized innuendo that the observational narration affords. Significantly enough, when young Corey has completed his mental revolution, he determines to make restitution and makes his way to Lapham's residence only to find him not at home. Thus, at the precise moment when Corey is ready to make amends to Lapham, Howells has already launched the Colonel on the downward financial ladder that will yet restore his integrity. Significantly too, Corey, having failed to connect with Lapham, finds Penelope at home and can thus declare his love to the astonished girl who, though she has known she has fallen in love with him, has assumed that he is in love with Irene. Love in this work is so encased in inhibitions that it can scarcely be expressed. As a result, relations between the sexes are not only misread by the parents; they are misread by the children of marriageable age. Such misreadings become on the one hand the devices by which Howells extends his plot and on the other a reflection of both the characters' and their author's inhibitions about love. Since the inhibition is so great, there is a sense that love is at once the underlying yet all but inexpressible motive behind both society and business, and is thus the deeper ground of embarrassment in Howells's world. Since it is inexpressible, a multitude of surface social and business actions are indirectly expressions of it, are in effect disguises of the erotic. Thus the most innocent exchanges, like the moment when Bartley feels the ball above Lapham's knee, are grounds for dis-ease. Similarly, the incident in which Corey, in a discussion with Irene at the new house, holds the tail of a carpenter's wood shaving while she thrusts her parasol tip through it, becomes an action that has provided a launching pad for a number of interpretive articles on the sexuality or lack of it being here expressed. We might say, following Trilling, that this is no more than a parasol being thrust through a shaving, yet the acute self-consciousness of the young couple, the shyness of the girl who is deliberately distracting herself in a preoccupation with the shaving, coupled with the context of hints, embarrassments, and innuendo combine to arouse in the reader a feel – there is no better word – for the hidden motives beneath the surplus inhibition.

Anxiety, inhibition, self-consciousness, and dis-ease all leading to embarrassment not only in the characters but in the reader – these are, if not the realism certainly the reality of the middle class world of William Dean Howells. There is no better perspective on this reality than that to be gained by turning once more to *The American*. Surely the most startling formal fact about the book is James's determination to remove Christopher Newman from the vernacular world from which, by any measure of verisimilitude, he should have his being. That this Western American self-made man with no formal education who has been engaged in the manufacture of washtubs should speak with the conversational aplomb of one born in a salon is enough to give us pause. Yet for all James's insistence on giving Newman the language of cultivated society, he is equally decisive in retaining his naïve identity as an unsophisticated American who, stretching himself to full length in the Louvre as if it were his private lounge, sees no difference between copy and original painting, who remains confident that his money can buy anything he wants, and who refers to acquiring a wife as getting the best article in the market. When he takes up his more or less permanent quarters in Paris, James makes clear that they are as garish as they are lavish. In the course of the novel he can be seen by a schooled social eye to make many blunders that mark his ignorance of genuine propriety.

Yet none of his lapses produce embarrassment to him or the reader. Even when Valentin is reduced to laughter at the sight of Newman's garish living quarters, the direction of the scene is not at all toward social shame but to a frank exchange on the part of both men. If James's decision to take Newman out of the American vernacular comes at a cost to the convention of social realism, it nonetheless releases his hero to make all that he can out of himself. By staying almost always at Newman's elbow in his narration, James remains in the immediate range of his expanding consciousness. That very expansion is itself an extension of the ac-

125

quisitive force that made him a successful businessman. If it exposes him to our reflective criticism, it does not interfere with our sense of his basic good nature. If there is an egoism in Newman's view of the world, there is nonetheless an abiding generosity in his spirit. That is why there is neither shame nor defiance about his innocence as there always is about Lapham's. If Newman is unsuccessful in possessing his Claire at the end of the novel, there remain both passion and good nature in his renunciation of revenge. It is interesting in this connection to remember that Howells, disappointed in the ending of *The American,* wished that James had worked toward a marriage between Newman and Claire. But James knew that just as Newman had renounced revenge on an old business enemy at the outset of the novel, he must renounce revenge at the end if he is to retain the good nature that is his trademark.

When we remember the freedom of language that Mark Twain gains through Huck's vernacular and the freedom of consciousness James achieves by getting his American out of the American vernacular, we are in a position to see the full constriction of the realistic middle class social space that Howells was determined to occupy. Whereas Huck Finn was in perpetual flight from the conscience that tyrannized over the civilized mind and James was attempting always to convert conscience and the fixed principles of morality into the fluidity of consciousness, Howells chose to remain precisely in the social realm where the conscience generated itself in the form of inhibitions. Thus, Silas Lapham, who in every way possesses the potentialities of the Emersonian self-reliant man, is at once contained and defeated by the society that Emerson exhorted his readers to scorn.

In his conception of Lapham, Howells clearly has Emerson in mind. The rough-hewn natural man arising from the raw materials of nature and seeming to bring with him a vernacular readiness for life, Lapham is set against the Coreys, who are just as clearly reflections of social overrefinement. Yet it cannot be argued that Lapham's honesty in the closing movement of the novel is in any way Emersonian. Lapham's redemption comes not from any transcendental vision but from an utterly conventional morality – morality upon which the Coreys and Bellinghams can place their seal of approval, which they duly do. They declare, in the light of Lapham's exemplary behavior, that he is a gentleman. More important than their declaration is the deeper logic of the novel indicating that Howells is somehow on *their* side. True, he sees the irony of their position and exposes them all along his way. But their language, their conversation, their social standing, their *society* is Howells's society. Insofar as he is not to the manner born, the very character of Silas Lapham is surely the measure of his resistance to that world. Yet if Lapham is in this sense an expression of Howells's criticism of cultivated society, there is nonetheless something in Lapham that Howells is ashamed of, embarrassed by.

Embarrassment is not a heroic emotion; it is essentially attendant upon insecurity and inhibition, and usually exploited in comedies of manners, a form in which Howells himself was adept. Yet *The Rise of Silas Lapham*, though hardly a tragedy, is nonetheless hardly a comedy of manners. It is a most ambitious attempt to discover the anxious reality of American middle class life. For Howells, the anxiety turns on inhibition and embarrassment. Yet embarrassment does not have to be identical with inhibition. Christopher Ricks in *Keats and Embarrassment*, his fine study of John Keats, discloses how Keats, whose life consisted in breaking through the ruthless class lines of English society, had tasted to the full the cup of shame and embarrassment awaiting those who made their way up from lower class status. Yet Keats also knew that the emotion was rooted in passion and eros, and some of his profoundest poetry bravely risked embarrassing lines in an effort to face down the inhibition and insecurity that both insulated and emasculated the throbbing heart of love. Keats fully appreciated Milton's line in which Adam tells Raphael of leading Eve "blushing like the Morn" to the nuptial bower; he recognized the two-handed strength that mastered both sides of the blush – its prelapsarian innocence and passion on the one hand and its potential shame and embarrassment after the fall on the other.

Howells stays firmly on one side of embarrassment – the side that is fallen and ashamed. Though he finally brings the children of the novel through to a marriage, their relationship is pervaded by inhibition. Mortified that Tom Corey loves her instead of her sister,

Penelope feels that her love can only wound the sister who had innocently yet fatuously thought that she was the object of his affection. Nothing can shake Penelope out of her shame, until Silas and Persis consult the Reverend Mr. Sewell, who advocates his economy of pain formula to them, which is to say that Penelope should marry Tom, leaving one person (Irene) miserable rather than all three. I realize that there are readers who find Mr. Sewell's formula bordering on wisdom, though it seems to me just one more part of Howells's attempt to achieve a balance of his moral books that still leaves a surplus of embarrassment intact. Even Mrs. Lapham recognizes that the formula is uttered by a man detached from the family dilemma. Nor does it really assuage the shame and misery that Penelope brings to the marriage. Presumably Tom Corey, who joins the West Virginia paint company, will bring to the marriage a measure of money and equanimity sufficient to allay the shame that the daughter of Lapham is prone to generate.

The essential truth of Sewell's vision in relation to the novel is that it turns not on pleasure but pain. Indeed, it comprehends a world of misery – not the misery of failure but the misery of success. It is a psychological misery bordering on neurosis. No wonder that Henry James blinked in astonishment at Howells's comparative popularity when he considered the essentially bleak portrait Howells painted of his middle class compatriots. In a deep way Howells seems to me not to have believed in love. Small wonder that he should be the first writer to take up the subject of divorce and make it the center of a novel. Even as he affirms marriage, he discloses that it is a relationship in which man and wife are ever so gently at each other's throats; they rub each other's conscience raw. At least they do if they are at the threshold of true upward mobility. Those who think that Sewell has achieved wisdom with his formula for economy of pain would do well to push on to *The Minister's Charge*, a subsequent Howells novel in which Mr. Sewell comes in for his share of embarrassment as he tries to sponsor a rough-hewn country boy's "entry" into Boston society. Doubly capitalizing on Sewell, Howells kept steadily at the business of writing. No wonder that Howells, when he was seventy, wrote to his brother that he felt that his writing "must have been done by a trust named after me."

Notes on Contributors

Paul A. Bové, a professor at the University of Pittsburgh, is the author of *Mastering Discourse, Intellectuals at War, Destructive Poetics,* and is currently writing a study of Henry Adams.

James M. Cox is a professor emeritus at Dartmouth College. He is the author of *Mark Twain: The Fate of Humor* and of numerous essays on American literature.

Wai-Chee Dimock is an associate professor at the University of California, San Diego. He is the author of *Empire for Liberty: Melville and the Poetics of Individualism*.

Daniel O'Hara, a professor at Temple University, is the author of *The Romance of Interpretation* and *Lionel Trilling: The Work of Liberation*.

Donald E. Pease holds the Ted and Helen Geisel Chair in the Humanities at Dartmouth College. He is the author of *Visionary Compacts: American Renaissance Writings in Cultural Contexts* and *Deterrence Pacts: Formation of the Canon in the Cold War Era*. He is also the editor of *American Renaissance Reconsidered; New Americanists: Revisionist Interventions into the Canon;* and, with Amy Kaplan, *Cultures of U.S. Imperialism*.

John Seelye, a professor at the University of Florida, is the author of *Prophetic Waters: The River in Early American Life and Literature* and is currently working on a sequel to that volume.

Selected Bibliography

Citations of *The Rise of Silas Lapham* in this book are to the Viking Penguin photo-offset reproduction of the text established by Walter J. Meserve and David J. Nordloh, published by the Indiana University Press in 1971 as Volume 12 of "A Selected Edition of W. D. Howells." That text is based on the *Century* serialized novel and was prepared according to procedures that the editors set forth in the textual apparatus (pp. 373–402) of the 1971 printing.

Bell, Michael Davitt. "The Sin of Art and the Problem of American Realism," *Prospects* 9 (1984): 115–42.

Berthoff, Warner. *The Ferment of Realism: American Literature 1884–1919*. New York: Macmillan, 1965.

Brodhead, Richard. "Hawthorne among the Realists: The Case of Howells." In Eric Sundquist, *American Realism: New Essays*. Baltimore: The Johns Hopkins University Press, 1982.

Cady, Edwin. *The Road to Realism: The Early Years, 1837–1885 of William Dean Howells*. Syracuse: Syracuse University Press, 1956.

The Realist at War: The Mature Years, 1885–1920 of William Dean Howells. Syracuse: Syracuse University Press, 1958.

Carrington, George. *The Immense Complex Drama: The World and Art of the Howells Novel*. Columbus: Ohio State University Press, 1966.

Chase, Richard. *The American Novel and Its Tradition*. Garden City, N.Y.: Doubleday, 1957.

Crowley, John W. *The Black Heart's Truth: The Early Career of W. D. Howells*. Chapel Hill: University of North Carolina Press, 1985.

Dooley, Patrick. "Nineteenth Century Business Ethics and *The Rise of Silas Lapham.*" *American Studies* 21 (1980).

Habegger, Alfred. *Gender, Fantasy and Realism in American Literature*. New York: Columbia University Press, 1982.

Howard, June. *Form and History in American Literary Nationalism*. Chapel Hill: University of North Carolina Press, 1985.

Kaplan, Amy. *The Social Construction of American Realism*. Chicago: University of Chicago Press, 1988, chapters 1 and 2.

131

Kazin, Alfred. *On Native Grounds: An Interpretation of Modern American Prose Literature.* New York: Anchor Books, 1959.

Kolb, Harold. *The Illusion of Life: American Realism as Literary Form.* Charlottesville: University Press of Virginia, 1969.

Lears, T. J. Jackson. *No Place of Grace: Antimodernism and the Transformation of American Culture, 1880–1920.* New York: Pantheon, 1981.

Lynn, Kenneth S. *William Dean Howells: An American Life.* New York: Harcourt Brace Jovanovich, 1971.

Martin, Jay. *Harvests of Change: American Literature, 1865–1914.* Englewood Cliffs, N.J.: Prentice-Hall, 1967.

Michaels, Walter Benn. "*Sister Carrie's* Popular Economy." *Critical Inquiry* 7 (1980): 373–90; reprinted as chapter 1 of *The Gold Standard and the Logic of Naturalism.* Berkeley: University of California Press, 1987.

Nettels, Elsa. *Language, Race and Social Class in Howells' America.* Louisville: University of Kentucky Press, 1988, pp. 153–62.

Parker, Gail Thain. "William Dean Howells: Realism and Feminism." In *Uses of Literature,* ed. Monroe Engel, *Harvard English Studies,* vol. 4 Cambridge, Mass.: Harvard University Press, 1973, pp. 133–62.

Pizer, Donald. *Realism and Naturalism in Nineteenth-Century American Literature.* Carbondale: Southern Illinois University Press, 1966.

Simpson, Lewis P. "The Treason of William Dean Howells." In *The Man of Letters in New England and the South: Essays on the History of Literary Vocation in America.* Baton Rouge: Louisiana State University Press, 1973.

Smith, Henry Nash. *Democracy and the American Novel: Popular Resistance to Classic American Writers.* New York: Oxford University Press, 1978.

Trachtenberg, Alan. *The Incorporation of America.* New York: Hill and Wang, 1982, chapter 6.

Vanderbilt, Kermit. *The Achievement of William Dean Howells.* Princeton, N.J.: Princeton University Press, 1968.

Wilson, Christopher. *The Labor of Words: Literary Professionalism in the Progressive Era.* Athens: University of Georgia Press, 1985.

"Markets and Fictions: Howells' Infernal Juggle," *American Literary Realism* 20 (1988): 2–22.